W9-BQY-124

The Supreme Court
and Public Prayer

God Who gave us life gave us liberty. Can the liberties of a nation be secure when we have removed a conviction that these liberties are the gift of God?

THOMAS JEFFERSON
Inscription on the
Thomas Jefferson Memorial,
Washington, D.C.

The Supreme Court and Public Prayer

The Need for Restraint

by

Charles E. Rice

Fordham University Press
New York

LIBRARY OF CONGRESS CATALOGUE CARD NUMBER: 64-18392

Acknowledgments

I wish to acknowledge the editorial assistance of Rev. Edwin A. Quain, S.J., whose comments were most helpful. Appreciation is also due especially to Mrs. Michael Suchy for her clerical preparation of the final manuscript, and to Mrs. James P. De Stefano and Miss Carmela Vassallo for their clerical assistance.

Contents

We have grown in numbers, wealth and power as no other nation has ever grown. But we have forgotten God . . . and we have vainly imagined, in the deceitfulness of our hearts, that all these blessings were produced by some superior wisdom and virtue of our own. Intoxicated with unbroken success, we have become too self-sufficient to feel the necessity of redeeming and preserving grace, too proud to pray to the God that made us. . . .

ABRAHAM LINCOLN
Proclamation of April 30, 1863

Preface

The school prayer decisions, handed down by the Supreme Court of the United States in 1962 and 1963, were wrongly decided.

In the prayer rulings, the Court paid an eccentric deference to the inflated scruples of a small minority, preferring them over the views of the vast majority who seek to extend to God a simple obeisance in accord with our national tradition. The Court quite naturally could find no solid foundations in history and legal precedent upon which to base this result. Instead, its reliance was largely upon abstract theories and, in the second decision, on a fragmented series of what lawyers call *obiter dicta*—general and even casual statements in Supreme Court opinions in previous cases, which statements were unnecessary to the decision of those cases and therefore are not valid as precedents binding the Court in subsequent cases.

The crucial point, making the decisions worth contesting, is that they have introduced a new conception of "neutrality" into the constitutional treatment of religion. Until 1962, the United States Constitution was concededly based upon a profession that, in fact, there is a God and there is a divine law to which men and nations are subject. In the school prayer cases, however, the Supreme Court denied that premise by enjoining upon government a rule of neutrality, in at least some situations, on the very question of whether there is a God at all.

The fact is that the Court thereby attempted a vain thing, for there can be no real neutrality on the basic religious question, "Is there a God?" The answer must be either a theistic "yes," an atheistic "no," or an agnostic "I don't know." All three, theism, atheism, and agnosticism are religions. The Court now has substituted for the traditional theistic premise a new agnostic premise entailing a perpetual suspension of judgment on the part of government as to the existence of God.

It is not fair to say that the Court has established an atheistic religion. Rather, the falsely neutral "agnosticism" is the watchword. Nor can we say that the Court has already removed, or that most of its members intend to remove, every trace of God from public life. Indeed, the Court majority has disclaimed any such intent. And it is definitely not a purpose of this book to draw into question in any way the good faith of the Justices of the Supreme Court. However, it is not too surprising that some, especially outside the legal profession, have done so in their perplexity at the rulings. An eminent commentator once remarked, with reference to the income tax decisions of the Supreme Court in the 1890's: "The question arises, how far a court is entitled to indulge in bad history and bad logic without having its good faith challenged. . . ."[1]

It remains to be seen whether the Court will be able to reject the extreme logical implications of its decisions when further extensions of the "neutrality" mandate are demanded by the vocal minority whose zeal for separation of church and state outruns its prudence and regard for the lessons of history and human nature. There are those, this writer among them, who are inclined to expect that the Court will find itself imprisoned by its logic, and that the American people will see most of the accustomed religious elements of public life eliminated singly but inexorably. Whether this development is in store, whether the Court will shrink from a logically consistent application of its reasoning, or whether a constitutional amendment will intervene, the school prayer controversy will have benefited the people through increasing their awareness of the need for religion in public as well as private life, and impressing upon them the evils attendant upon an excursion

1. Edward S. Corwin, *Court Over Constitution* (New York, 1950), 188.

by the Supreme Court beyond its passive function of judging to an active role as a conscious, willful agent of fundamental change.

If the school prayer cases have the effect of erecting agnosticism as the official religion of American public life, the event will have consequences beyond the violence done to the letter and spirit of the First Amendment. The United States of America are locked in a struggle which can issue in the triumph or extinction of liberty throughout the world. The conflict, moreover, is one of spiritual as well as material dimensions. Indeed, the apocalyptic nature of the cold war follows from the fact that it involves a collision of irreconcilably contradictory philosophies as to the nature of man himself.

The West (and I do not restrict the term to the geographically western nations) is the repository of the traditional Christian beliefs that men are made for a destiny higher than this life, "that they are endowed by their Creator with certain unalienable Rights," and that a primary purpose of government is, in the phrase of the Declaration of Independence, "to secure these Rights." Communism, by contrast, relies upon the assumptions that there is no God and that man and all else in the world are purely material. You cannot analyze a spiritual thing under a microscope. You cannot predict precisely what a spiritual soul will do. But if you are dealing with a material thing, such as this paper, you can analyze it completely, you can see what makes it work, and you can predict exactly what it will do under any given circumstances. So with the human being and society. The Communist has put them under a dialectical microscope and, because he regards them as wholly material, he has reached conclusions as to the future of man and society which are as certain to the Communist as is the conclusion that this paper would burn if placed in a fire. In a word, the Communist vision sees the world inevitably moving, with revolution as midwife, toward the dictatorship of the proletariat, or socialist society, which will ultimately usher in the final historical stage of the Communist society, in which there will be no private property, and therefore no classes (because, in the Communist view, it is the existence of private property that has divided society into classes), and finally the state itself will wither away (because the only function of the state, in Communist terms, is to be an instrument for the suppression of other classes by the dominant class.) It must be remembered that the withering away of the state, which is the ultimate goal of Communism, can never fully occur as long as there are capitalist-imperialist nations which are, by definition, irreconcilably hostile to the socialist states. This is so because the existence of capitalist-imperialist nations requires the maintenance of a strong socialist state for at least defensive purposes. A world-wide revolution, therefore, is inherent in the Communist order of reality.

It is most important here that the basic premises of Communism are its denials of God and the spiritual nature of man. From these postulates follow the messianic nature of Communism and the irreconcilability of its struggle with the West. In these premises we find the basic conflict between Communism and the West. Nor can we belittle the Communist doctrine by saying that it is only a species of campaign oratory used to cover a conventional imperialistic urge on the part of its leaders. In the words of Rev. John Courtney Murray, S.J., "the Soviet Empire not only has been, and is, an empire controlled by doctrine, but must continue to be such, on peril of ceasing to be itself."[2]

It is given to the United States, at this moment in history, to wage the struggle on behalf of freedom and against Communist tyranny. The job can be adequately done only if this nation, as the leader of the free world, articulates the case for liberty in its essential elements. This requires an affirmation that indeed there is a God, that He has endowed men with unalienable rights and that even the state is subject to His law. For more than one reason, therefore, the recent Supreme Court decisions are disturbing. They have been justly criticized as inferior constitutional craftsmanship, erecting the private abstractions of the Justices to the rank of constitutional imperatives, and doing so with a disregard for history, common sense and the lessons of experience. But it is even more disturbing, and dangerous, that the rulings appear to fasten an agnostic orthodoxy upon the government of the

2. John Courtney Murray, *We Hold These Truths* (New York, 1960), 233.

United States. They seem to have enjoined that the government shall maintain a perpetual suspension of judgment on all questions of God, including the very basic question of whether He even exists.

As an American, I cannot help resenting the school prayer decisions, because, in their refusal to affirm that the Creator is the source of the rights of man, they give the lie to the birth certificate of my nation—the Declaration of Independence. What is more, I fear them because they tend to disarm my country in the face of an implacable and powerful foe, whose greatest strength is his unswerving adherence to a materialistic faith. The school prayer decisions, and the future inroads on religious liberty that may come in their wake, pose a threat to the welfare and security of the United States. With the vast majority of the American people, I believe that our character as a nation under God must be preserved, and that the pretensions of those who would deconsecrate this nation must be emphatically and permanently rebuffed. Only if we continue to draw upon the religious wellsprings of our greatness can we hope to fulfill our national destiny.

Fortunately, an effort is being made, in Congress and elsewhere, to check the agnostic trend of the Court through the enactment of a constitutional amendment, not to change the Constitution, but to restore it, to repair the breach opened by the federal judiciary which Thomas Jefferson described as "the subtle corps of sappers and miners constantly working underground to undermine the foundations of the confederate fabric."[3] It is my hope that this book will contribute something to the general discussion and consensus that are needed for the solution of our difficulty. It does not pretend to be comprehensive, nor is it exhaustive. Rather, it is a statement of a position shared by many, buttressed by what I believe are relevant considerations of history, law and reason.

3. *The Writings of Thomas Jefferson,* Albert E. Bergh, ed. (Washington, D.C.), XV, 297.

. . . reason and experience forbid us to expect that national morality can prevail in exclusion of religious principle.

GEORGE WASHINGTON
Farewell Address

I

What Did the Court Do?

Few will dissent from the proposition that a sound national morality ought to prevail, but many will disagree as to the way it should be promoted. Washington's Farewell Address is justly regarded as a catalogue of sensible advice for the commonwealth he had done so much to create. Some of his recommendations, however, have been disregarded under the influence of modern events. An example is his warning against entangling alliances. The current trend of the Supreme Court indicates that also Washington's predication of national (including public as well as private) morality upon religious principle is no longer safe as a verity of American life.

This incipient change was brought sharply to the fore on June 25, 1962, when the Supreme Court, in the case of *Engel v. Vitale*,[1] decided that the recitation, as part of a public school program, of the twenty-two-word New York State Regents' Prayer, is unconstitutional, even though students were not required to participate in the recitation. The five petitioners—two of the Jewish faith, one a member of the Society for Ethical Culture, one Unitarian and one "non-believer"—were parents of public school children and they objected to the procedure and sought to compel the discontinuance of the prayer. The prayer read: "Almighty God, we acknowledge our dependence upon Thee, and we beg thy blessings upon us, our parents, our teachers and our country."

The First Amendment religion clauses provide: "Congress shall make no law respecting an establishment of religion, or prohibiting the free exercise thereof. . . ." The Fourteenth Amendment, adopted in 1868, provides that no State may ". . . deprive any person of life, liberty, or property, without due process of law. . . ." The Court had held, prior to the school prayer cases, that the Fourteenth Amendment subjected the states to the restrictions which the First Amendment had applied to the federal government. The states thereby were forbidden, as was Congress, from making any "law respecting an establishment of religion, or prohibiting the free exercise thereof. . . ." Thus the Court in 1962 held that, by instituting the Regents' Prayer, New York had violated the establishment clause of the First Amendment by enacting a "law respecting an establishment of religion."

It must be remembered that the Regents' Prayer was composed by state officials and so the Engel decision did not of itself hold unconstitutional all prayers in public schools. However, Mr. Justice Black, for the six-man majority of the Court, went afield to warn that a governmental prescription of "any particular form of prayer"[2] would be objectionable, apparently regardless of authorship. Nor was the Regents' Prayer the first example of government-written prayer in this country. Chaplains in the armed forces compose prayers, and even the prayer, "God save the United States and this Honorable Court," with which the bailiff opens each session of the Supreme Court of the United States, was written by an official on the public payroll. Mr. Justice Douglas, in his concurring opinion, labeled these and similar practices unconstitutional. Mr. Justice Stewart dissented from the majority opinion of five justices. Justices Frankfurter and White did not participate in the case.

Criticism of the Supreme Court and its decisions has a definite value as well as a long and honorable history. The late Chief Justice Harlan F. Stone observed:

> When the courts deal, as ours do, with great public questions, the only protection against unwise decisions, and even judicial usurpation, is careful scrutiny of their action and fearless comment upon it.

In the school prayer matter, comment, fearless and otherwise, appeared without delay. Numerous senators and congressmen attacked the Engel decision. So, of course, did clergymen. The ruling, said Cardinal Spellman, "strikes at the very heart of the godly tradition in which America's children have for so long been raised." Episcopal Bishop James A. Pike protested that the Court had "deconsecrated" the nation. The trend evidenced by the decision involves us in a "travesty," brought on "through an essentially thought-denying absolutist approach," later observed Harvard Law School Dean Erwin N. Griswold.

Others, however, supported the decision in varying degrees. President Kennedy scrupulously avoided any condemnation of the ruling, urged the people to pray at home and exhorted them to continue to support the Supreme Court. Mr. Leo Pfeffer, General Counsel of the American Jewish Congress, exulted that "this decision makes it clear that all religious practices in the public schools, such as Bible reading, prayer recitation and religious holiday observances, are unconstitutional. It also makes it clear that neither Federal nor state funds may constitutionally be used for the support of parochial schools." The Baptist General Convention of Texas agreed with the Court that "there is no place in American life for prayers formulated by the Government." The action of the Court in banning the prayer was editorially hailed by the *Hindustani Times,* of New Delhi, India, as "one of the finest examples of secularism in practice," and "relevant to India where the implications of secularism have yet to be widely understood." The Communist party of the United States, ever ready to fish in troubled waters, headlined the July 1st, 1962, editorial in *The Worker,* "A Patriotic Decision," and described the ruling as a "powerful affirmation of the inviolability of the First Amendment."

The controversy finally became so acute that Mr. Justice Clark, who had joined in the opinion of the Court, made an unusual public statement emphasizing the limited scope and reach of the actual decision. It is rare for a sitting Justice of the Supreme Court to comment publicly on a case in such a manner. The Senate Committee on the Judiciary initiated hearings on several proposed constitutional amendments to reverse the decision. But there were no similar hearings then in the House Committee on the Judiciary.

It came as no surprise when the Court, in June, 1963, invalidated the use of the Lord's Prayer and readings from the Bible as devotional exercises in public schools. The cases, entitled *School District of Abington Township v. Schempp* and *Murray v. Curlett,* arose in Pennsylvania and Maryland. In the Maryland case, Mrs. Madalyn Murray, a militant atheist, protested in her own right and in behalf of her sixteen-year-old son, who attended a public school and was an atheist, against the practice in the Baltimore public schools of opening each school morning with a reading from the King James version of the Bible. The Philadelphia complaint was made by Mr. and Mrs. Edward L. Schempp, for themselves and their children who attended a public high school, to enjoin the opening of the school day with a public reading by students from various versions of the Bible and the recitation of the Lord's Prayer. The Schempps were Unitarians. In both cases, provision was made for excusal of objecting children. Mrs. Murray and her son, nevertheless, objected that the practice "subjects their freedom of conscience to the rule of the majority."[3] Mr. Schempp testified that he feared that his children would be "labeled as 'odd balls' " on account of their nonparticipation.[4] The cases were disposed of in a single decision, with Mr. Justice Clark, speaking for the Court,[5] saying that the practices violated the First Amendment command that government shall be "neutral" in matters of religion. Justices Douglas, Brennan, Goldberg and Harlan concurred in the decision and Mr. Justice Stewart again was the lone dissenter. For convenience, we shall refer to this as the Schempp case.

Perhaps because it was expected, the Schempp decision did not provoke the spontaneous public outrage that greeted the Regents' Prayer decision. To be sure, the ruling was denounced, but the criticism, while strenuous, was countered by a substantial number of statements in favor of the Court's action. The Rev. Dr. Billy Graham said he was "shocked" at the decision. Bishop Fred Pierce Corson, President of the

World Methodist Council, voiced his opinion that the decision does not accord with the "law of the land." Approval of the decision, however, was voiced by the Rev. Dr. Eugene Carson Blake, head of the United Presbyterian Church, Rabbi Uri Miller, President of the Synagogue Council of America, and other representatives of liberal Protestant communities and some Jewish organizations. The president and general secretary of the National Council of Churches viewed the ruling as a reminder that "teaching religious commitment is the responsibility of the home and the community of faith, such as the church or synagogue, rather than the public schools. . . ." On the other hand, Roman Catholic Cardinals Spellman, McIntyre and Cushing, in Rome to elect a new Pope, vigorously scored the decision. Conservative Protestant spokesmen, such as the Rt. Rev. Leland Stark, Bishop of the Protestant Episcopal Diocese of Newark, also deplored the action of the Court.

Congressional reaction, perhaps because of the brooding and distracting problem of civil rights, was not as violent as the previous year. Even so, there was much criticism in Congress, and numerous constitutional amendments were proposed. No action has yet been taken on any of them.

One unanswered question, of course, is the extent to which local communities and school officials will comply with the mandate of the Court. On the very day of the Schempp ruling, the Superintendent of Education of South Carolina announced that his state would ignore the decision. North Carolina, Alabama and Mississippi promptly followed suit. If such an attitude were to spread, the difficulties of enforcement would be obvious. So too would be the decline of the Supreme Court as a conceded and final arbiter of basic constitutional issues. The general reaction among the states, however, was mixed, with most undertaking in various ways to comply with the ruling. Massachusetts immediately went so far as to cancel previously scheduled prayers at public school graduation exercises. But an undercurrent of dissatisfaction was evidenced in at least nine states by state authorities and local school boards which adopted a variety of tactics to delay or circumvent the application of the ruling.[6]

WHAT THE DECISIONS MEAN

It will be helpful here to pause and consider exactly what the Supreme Court had previously held in those cases cited as precedent for the ruling in the Schempp case. Each of those prior cases involved a challenge to a governmental program on the ground that it violated either the First Amendment prohibition of an establishment of religion, or the free exercise of religion guaranteed by that Amendment. As we review them, let us consider the nature of the program in each case and its surrounding circumstances, what it was that the complainants sought to accomplish by the litigation, what the Supreme Court actually decided, and what extraneous statements, or *obiter dicta* in the lawyers' phrase, were so used by the Court or some of its members as to provide a springboard for decisions in later cases.

A New Jersey statute authorizing school districts to provide transportation for children to and from school was contested in *Everson v. Board of Education*[7] in 1947. Acting pursuant to the statute, the board of education of Ewing Township authorized reimbursement to parents of money expended by them for the transportation of their children to and from school on regular buses operated by the public transportation system. Part of this reimbursement was to parents for their expenditure of money for the transportation of their children attending Roman Catholic parochial schools. The complainant, a taxpayer of the school district, sued to prevent reimbursement by the board of the parents of parochial school students, alleging that it was a "law respecting an establishment of religion" and therefore violated the First Amendment. The Supreme Court rejected this contention, in a five-to-four decision, with Mr. Justice Black for the five-man majority emphasizing that the statute served primarily a public purpose by helping children get safely to and from school. The assistance it provided to church schools and their pupils was held to be a permissible incidental effect. The Court in Everson, however, went beyond the necessities of the case and, through the pen of Justice Black, the majority framed a sweeping description of the effect of the establishment clause—a description which was to serve as a semantic springboard for the questionable decisions to follow:

> The "establishment of religion" clause of the First Amendment means at least this: Neither a state nor the Federal Government can set up a church. *Neither can pass laws which aid one religion, aid all religions, or prefer one religion over another.* Neither can force nor influence a person to go to or to remain away from church against his will or force him to profess a belief or disbelief in any religion. No person can be punished for entertaining or professing religious beliefs or disbeliefs, for church attendance or non-attendance. No tax in any amount, large or small, can be levied to support any religious activities or institutions, whatever they may be called, or whatever form they may adopt to teach or practice religion. Neither a state nor the Federal Government can, openly or secretly, participate in the affairs of any religious organizations or groups and vice versa. In the words of Jefferson, the clause against establishment of religion by law was intended to erect "a wall of separation between church and state[8] (Italics added).

Despite this broad language, it must be remembered that the Court (and Justice Black), in Everson actually held that the New Jersey bus plan was constitutional. The holding of the case, however, has been overshadowed by its rhetoric. One year later, in 1948, the Supreme Court relied on that Everson dictum of Justice Black to declare unconstitutional the "released time" program of religious education in the public schools of Champaign, Illinois.[9] In 1940, members of the Jewish, Roman Catholic, and some of the Protestant faiths, had formed a voluntary association called the Champaign Council on Religious Education. They obtained permission from the Board of Education to offer religious instructions to public school pupils, whose parents requested that they attend, in the public school classrooms for one period a week. The religious teachers were employed by the Council at no expense to the school authorities, although they were subject to the approval and supervision of the superintendent of schools. Students who did not take the religious instruction were required to leave their classrooms and go to a designated place in the school building to pursue secular studies. Students who did enroll for the religious classes were required to attend, and absences were reported to the school authorities just as they would be for secular classes. Mrs. Vashti McCollum, whose sixteen-year-old son was a public school student, objected to the program and brought suit to force its discontinuance. Mrs. McCollum, incidentally, is now President of the American Humanist Association. The Illinois courts upheld the released-time program, but the Supreme Court reversed them by an eight to one vote, with Justice Stanley Reed dissenting. Significantly, the Court quoted the broad Everson dictum in full[10] and rejected the board of education's contention "that historically the First Amendment was intended to forbid only government preference of one religion over another, not an impartial governmental assistance of all religions."[11] As we shall see in Chapters II and III, the Court's historical conclusion on this point was incorrect. The Court, through Justice Black, concluded in the McCollum case:

> Here not only are the State's tax-supported public school buildings used for the dissemination of religious doctrines. The State also affords sectarian groups an invaluable aid in that it helps to provide pupils for their religious classes through use of the State's compulsory public school machinery. This is not separation of Church and State.[12]

The Court felt that such public assistance to religious groups violated the Constitution because, "as we said in the Everson case, the First Amendment has erected a wall between Church and State which must be kept high and impregnable."[13] In a significant concurring opinion in the McCollum case, Justice Frankfurter underscored the limited actual reach of the ruling, emphasizing that some forms of released time programs might well be unobjectionable.[14] Justices Jackson, Rutledge and Burton joined in the Frankfurter opinion.

The McCollum decision met a storm of opposition, especially from organized churches. Particularly strong criticism was directed against the Court's erroneous rejection of the argument that the First Amendment was intended to forbid only governmental preference of one religion over another. The Court's explicit refusal in McCollum to approve, even in principle, impartial governmental assistance to all religions caused fear that governmental accommodation of religion was giving way to a Court-ordained hostility. But four years later, in 1952, the Court retrenched by upholding the New York City "dismissed time" program of religious instruction for public school students. Under that plan the public schools released their pupils for a period during the school day, on written request of the parents, so that they could go to churches or church schools for religious instruction. Students not so released remained at their secular studies in the public school, and the churches reported to the public school authorities the names of pupils who failed to report for religious instruction. The Supreme Court, in the case of *Zorach v. Clauson,* approved the plan by a six to three vote, with Justices Black, Frankfurter and Jackson dissenting.[15] Mr. Justice Douglas, for the majority of the Court, ruled that the complaining parents had not shown that their children were coerced, and then attempted to distinguish the case from McCollum:

> In the McCollum case, the classrooms were used for religious instruction and the force of the public school was used to promote that instruction. Here, as we have said, the public schools do no more than accommodate their schedules to a program of outside religious instruction. We follow the McCollum case. But we cannot expand it to cover the present released time program unless separation of Church and State means that public institutions can make no adjustments of their schedules to accommodate the religious needs of the people. We cannot read into the Bill of Rights such a philosophy of hostility to religion.[16]

The two major factual distinctions between McCollum and Zorach are that in Zorach the religious instructions were held outside of public property and in Zorach there was lacking any element of coercion of the children, an element which the McCollum Court seemed to feel was implicit in that case. The Zorach case is particularly interesting for several reasons. For one thing, although the Court pulled away from the extreme implications of McCollum, it did not wholly abandon the absolutist principles born in the Everson case five years earlier. In a passage for which he cited the McCollum and Everson cases as authority, Justice Douglas, speaking for the Court in Zorach, said:

> There cannot be the slightest doubt that the First Amendment reflects the philosophy that Church and State should be separated. And so far as interference with the "free exercise" of religion and an "establishment" of religion are concerned, the separation must be complete and unequivocal.[17]

But the case is noteworthy also because Justice Douglas expressed a far more realistic attitude toward church-state cooperation than he was later to evidence in the school prayer cases. For instance, in his Zorach opinion, he continued, after the sweeping generalizations just quoted, by voicing these qualifications:

> The First Amendment, however, does not say that in every and all respects there shall be a separation of Church and State. Rather, it studiously defines the manner, the specific ways, in which there shall be no concert or union or dependency one on the other. That is the common sense of the matter. Otherwise the state and religion would be aliens to each other—hostile, suspicious, and even unfriendly. Churches could not be required to pay even property taxes. Municipalities would not be permitted to render police or fire protection to religious groups. Policemen who helped parishioners into their places of worship would violate the Constitution. Prayers in our legislative halls; the appeals to the Almighty in the messages of the Chief Executive; the proclamations making Thanksgiving Day a holiday; "so help me God" in our courtroom oaths—these and all other references to the Almighty that run through our laws, our public rituals, our ceremonies would be flouting the First Amendment. *A fastidious atheist or agnostic could even object to the supplication with which the Court opens each session:* "God save the United States and this Honorable Court"[18] (Italics added).

It is, of course, an overstatement to say that the rather spartan language of the two religion clauses of the First Amendment "studiously defines the manner, the specific ways" in which church and state shall be separate. In the Regents' Prayer case in 1962, Mr. Justice Douglas clearly indicated his belief that most of the practices enumerated in this passage, including the supplication at the opening of each session of the Supreme Court, are unconstitutional.[19] Surely, he did not intend to classify himself as a "fastidious atheist or agnostic," which he is not, and the implication is not a necessary one. He did not say that "only" a fastidious atheist or agnostic could object to the supplication. In any event, there is no doubt that Justice Douglas's moderate and practical ruling in the Zorach case, in which he also observed, "We are a religious people whose institutions presuppose a Supreme Being,"[20] is surely preferable to the rigid abstractions of the school prayer cases.

The fact that the wide-ranging dictum of the Everson case had survived the Zorach retreat unscathed was underscored in the 1961 cases in which the Supreme Court upheld several Sunday-closing laws. In those cases, the Court sustained the Maryland,[21] Pennsylvania,[22] and Massachusetts[23] laws against the objections that they were laws respecting an establishment of religion and that they impinged on the free exercise of religion by merchants whose religious faith dictated that they observe Saturday as the Sabbath and who were thus required by the Sunday-closing laws to close their shops two days a week. In rejecting these objections, and holding that there was no denial of equal protection of the laws to such merchants, the Court, with Chief Justice Warren announcing the judgment in each case, emphasized that the Sunday-closing laws had evolved beyond their religious origins and had simply become secular statutes mandating one day of rest in seven. As such they were reasonable and valid, despite the incidental burden imposed upon Sabbatarians and the incidental benefit to organized religions. The case of *McGowan v. Maryland* was the one of the four in which the various Justices explored in depth the meaning of the First Amendment guarantees. Significantly, in his opinion for the Court in that case, the Chief Justice quoted approvingly, fully—and unnecessarily—the sweeping Everson dictum describing the reach of the establishment clause.[24] And although the Court found the Sunday-closing laws to be justified as non-religious public welfare legislation, the Everson dictum was given renewed vigor.

Less than a month later, the Supreme Court relied again upon the Everson dictum in holding unconstitutional the provision of the Maryland Constitution requiring state employees to declare their belief in the existence of God.[25] When Roy R. Torcaso, a citizen and resident of Maryland, was denied a commission as a notary public because he refused to make the declaration, he sued the clerk of the local court to compel the issuance of the commission to him regardless of the constitutional requirement. The Maryland courts denied him relief, but the Supreme Court of the United States, without dissent, reversed and ordered that the commission be issued. The Court, through Mr. Justice Black, held that the oath requirement was an invasion of Torcaso's "freedom of belief and religion."[26] It is not clear whether the Court considered the oath to violate the establishment clause or the free exercise clause of the First Amendment, or both. We shall analyze in Chapter IV the Court's ruling in the Torcaso case that the oath violated the First Amendment command that government shall be neutral among religions. But it is important here to note that Justice Black, for the Court in Torcaso, relied heavily upon the now-celebrated Everson dictum, and upon a rhetorical statement by Justice Frankfurter in his concurring opinion in the McCollum case:

> We are all agreed that the First and Fourteenth Amendments have a secular reach far more penetrating in the conduct of Government than merely to forbid an "established church." . . . We renew our conviction that 'we have staked the very existence of our country on the faith that complete separation between the state and religion is best for the state and best for religion.'[27]

And so the stage was set for the school prayer cases. It is significant to note the endurance of the Everson dictum, for its continuing acceptance by the Court (although no case was specifically cited in the 1962 Regents' Prayer case), signalled the adoption by that body of the concept that government cannot aid all religions impartially. This concept carries within itself, perhaps irrepressibly, the seeds of governmental hostility to religion. And while we can justly criticize the Court's readiness to rely upon *obiter dicta*—extraneous and often rhetorical statements in prior cases—the more basic difficulty lies in the nature of the *dicta* relied upon, that is, in their full-blown rejection of the practical rule that the establishment clause was designed to prevent governmental favoritism among sects and was not aimed at impartial governmental assistance to, or accommodation of, religion and religious groups. As we shall see in Chapter IV, this error is compounded by an even graver mistake—the expansion of the concept of neutrality to mean that government shall be completely neutral as between religions that believe in God and those that do not so believe.

Before discussing whether the two school prayer decisions are consistent with the letter and spirit of the Constitution, as well as with American tradition, it is important to note what the Court actually did in each case and some of the reasons advanced by the Justices.

Engel v. Vitale, the Regents' Prayer case of 1962, was one of those rare cases in which the opinion of the Court did not cite a single case in its support. Rather, its reliance was upon abstract logic and such historical materials as James Madison's *Memorial and Remonstrance,* which we shall discuss on pages 33 and 45, and the Book of Common Prayer of the Church of England, which a generous analysis can describe as only marginally relevant. The absence of legal citations in *Engel v. Vitale* has been hailed as evidence of the pristine purity of the principles there avowed, the lofty eminence of which precludes their dependence upon mere court decisions. On the other hand, it can fairly be said that the Court cited no precedent because it could find none beyond its own gratuitous *dicta* in prior cases since 1947. The ruling truly was unexampled and unprecedented, although it was not unexpected.

In *Engel v. Vitale,* the Supreme Court really did no more than strike down a prayer *written* by public officials (The New York State Board of Regents) for recital as part of a religious program carried on by government. But Mr. Justice Black, speaking for the majority of the Court, foreshadowed the result in the Bible reading and Lord's Prayer cases when he noted that "each separate government in this country should stay out of the business of writing *or sanctioning* official prayers and leave that purely religious function to the people themselves and to those the people choose to look to for religious guidance"[28] (Italics added). One year later, in the 1963 Schempp case, Mr. Justice Clark rested his opinion for the Court on "the concept of neutrality,"[29] which operates to prevent a situation where the "official support of the state or federal government would be placed behind the tenets of one *or all* orthodoxies"[30] (Italics added.)

In the Engel case, the Court did not emphasize greatly the idea of government neutrality among religions, but rather seemed to rest upon an assumed incapacity of government, under the First Amendment, to conduct or sponsor "religious services"[31] of any type, at least in public schools. The Engel Court did not dwell upon the reason for such an incapacity. But the reason was intimated by Mr. Justice Black, speaking for the majority of the Court, when he noted in passing: "When the power, prestige and financial support of government is placed behind a particular religious belief, the indirect coercive pressure upon religious minorities to conform to the prevailing *officially approved religion* is plain"[32] (Italics added). What Justice Black hinted at here was the same concept of neutrality which was later explicitly found controlling in the Schempp case.

It is fair to conclude, therefore, that the ultimate rationale of both decisions is a First Amendment command of governmental neutrality in religious matters, a rationale implied in Engel and specifically advanced in Schempp. It remains to ask what is the nature of the required neutrality. What test can be used to see if the government is being neutral? It is too early to tell with precision, and we shall have to await further decisions. But we can say that government will breach its duty of neutrality, according to the Schempp Court, if it performs or sponsors a "religious exercise," or if it enacts a law affecting religion, financially or otherwise, that has no secular legislative purpose or that has "a primary effect" that "advances" or "inhibits" religion.[33]

The Regents' Prayer, Bible reading and the Lord's Prayer all were invalidated because they were government-sponsored "religious exercises," and the Court did not have to go further and find expressly that they constituted unconstitutional financial support of religion. The financial support prohibition, however, may be of even greater significance than the bar against government sponsorship of religious exercises. It is important, therefore, to examine the way the Supreme Court regards financial support as a possible violation of neutrality. Thus, in the passage quoted above, Mr. Justice Black spoke of "the power, prestige and *financial support* of government"[34] (Italics added) being placed behind an officially approved religion. Mr. Justice Douglas, in his concurring opinion in Engel, put it squarely: "The point for decision is whether the Government can constitutionally finance a religious exercise."[35] He reiterated this position in his concurring opinion in the Schempp case. In Schempp, Mr. Justice Clark, after recounting some opinions in prior Court cases, spoke of the "wholesome 'neutrality' of which this Court's cases speak. . . ."[36] But the prior opinions to which he referred were ones in which the prohibition of financial support of any or all religions is a recurring theme. For example, the extracts from past opinions which the Schempp Court thus approvingly quoted included the following:

> Neither a state nor the Federal Government can set up a church. Neither can pass laws which aid one religion, *aid all religions,* or prefer one religion over another. (Italics added.)[37] (The Schempp opinion cited this passage to show that "this Court has rejected unequivocally the contention that the establishment clause forbids only governmental preference of one religion over another.")[38]

> The effect of the First Amendment was to take every form of propagation of religion out of the realm of things which could *directly or indirectly be made public business* and thereby be supported in whole or in part *at taxpayers' expense.* . . . This freedom was first in the Bill of Rights because it was first in the forefathers' minds; it was set forth in absolute terms, and its strength is its rigidity[39] (Italics added).

> The (First) Amendment's purpose . . . was to create a complete and permanent separation of the spheres of religious activity and civil authority by comprehensively *forbidding every form of public aid or support for religion*[40] (Italics added).

> Our constitutional policy . . . (D) oes not deny the value or necessity for religious training, teaching or observance. Rather it secures their free exercise. But to that end *it does deny that the state can undertake or sustain them in any form or degree.* For this reason the sphere of religious activity, as distinguished from the secular intellectual liberties, has been given the two-fold protection and, as the state cannot forbid, *neither can it perform or aid in performing the religious function.* The dual prohibition makes that function altogether private[41] (Italics added).

> Separation is a requirement to abstain from fusing functions of Government and of religious sects, not merely to treat them all equally.[42]

> We repeat and again reaffirm that neither a State nor the Federal Government can constitutionally force a person "to profess a belief or disbelief in any religion." Neither can constitutionally pass laws or impose requirements which *aid all religions as against non-believers, and neither can aid those religions based on a belief in the existence of God as against those religions founded on different beliefs*[43] (Italics added).

> When the power, prestige and *financial support* of government is placed behind a particular religious belief, the indirect coercive pressure upon religious minorities to conform to the prevailing officially approved religion is plain[44] (Italics added).

Financial support of any or all religions, therefore, may easily breach the rule of neutrality and run afoul of the First Amendment. The Court in the Schempp decision then prescribed a test which seems to apply to enactments relating to religious exercises as well as those providing financial support of religion:

> The test may be stated as follows: what are the purpose and the primary effect of the enactment? If either is the advancement or inhibition of religion then the enactment exceeds the scope of legislative power as circumscribed by the Constitution. That is to say that to withstand the strictures of the Establishment Clause there must be a secular legislative purpose and a primary effect that neither advances nor inhibits religion.[45]

For this proposition, the Court cited *Everson v. Board of Education* (1947) and *McGowan v. Maryland* (1961), which cases we have discussed on pages 8 and 13.

What, then, is disturbing about the school prayer decisions? For one thing, they have introduced a dogmatic interdiction against governmental conduct or sponsorship of religious exercises that is more rigid than anything heretofore conceived, and which will be difficult to confine. The American Civil Liberties Union in Los Angeles, promptly after the Schempp decision, filed suit to remove the words "under God" from the pledge of allegiance. Mr. Justice Douglas agrees with them. If the words constitute a "religious exercise," the majority of the Court would also seem to agree. Mr. Justice Brennan labored mightily for 74 pages in his concurring opinion in the Schempp case to forestall any suspicion that the ruling would be pushed to extreme limits. Yet the best he could do on the pledge of allegiance was to say: "The reference to divinity in the revised pledge of allegiance, for example, may merely recognize the historical fact that our Nation *was believed to have been founded 'under God.'*"[46] (Italics added.) Congress, as a matter of fact, had inserted the words "under God" into the pledge in 1954, and the Report of the House Committee on the Judiciary emphatically asserted in the present tense "the dependence of our people and our Government upon the moral directions of the Creator."[47] Mr. Justice Brennan similarly dismissed any thought that the inscription, "In God We Trust," which was made the national motto by Act of Congress in 1956, is necessarily unconstitutional. This practice, he noted, is not insignificant but it has ceased to have *religious meaning,* and *therefore* is unobjectionable. Apparently, the price of retaining religious references in our public life is an agreement that they are not to be taken seriously. This problem is discussed on page 109.

Probably the most disturbing aspect of the school prayer decisions is the Court's total adoption of the notion that government must be neutral as between religions which acknowledge a belief in God and those non-theistic religions, such as Ethical Culture and Secular Humanism, which do not admit the existence of God. Formerly, the First Amendment concept of neutrality left room for government to acknowledge the existence and sovereignty of God, while maintaining a practical impartiality among the various theistic creeds and avoiding coercion of any, whether believers or not. Now, it appears that the Court has enjoined upon government a perpetual suspension of judgment even on the question of God's existence. It will be difficult for the Court to draw the line. The references to God in the pledge of allegiance, the national motto, the national anthem, etc., cannot really be dismissed under the maxim, *de minimis non curat lex*—the law will not concern itself with trifles. Mr. Justice Brennan in the Schempp case specifically said this maxim does not apply to "In God We Trust" as a motto or inscription.[48] Nor did Mr. Justice Black, for the Court in Engel, apply the maxim to such things, but rather he found them unobjectionable because they are merely "patriotic or ceremonial" and encourage the expression only of "love for our country."[49] The implication is plain in all this that any governmental encouragement of love or reverence for God as well as our country is unconstitutional if it is seriously meant, no matter how minor the occasion or how general the encouragement. It will be constitutional only if it is not meant to be believed—one might say only if it is hypocrisy. This question will be discussed further on page 112.

A third troublesome feature of the school prayer decisions is that the Court may now be about to broaden the concept of financial support, to invalidate practices heretofore concededly constitutional. The tax benefits accorded to religious bodies, such as the exemption of churches from real property taxes and the deduction for contributions to churches, are thought by Mr. Justice Douglas to be invalid, and the broad language of the opinion of the court in Schempp may require that result. Mr. Justice Brennan's justification of this practice as an incidental benefit which is available to all religious bodies, theistic and non-theistic, without discrimination, does not fully adhere to the rule of the majority in Schempp, that an enactment aiding religion, to be constitutional, must have "a secular legislative purpose and a primary effect that neither advances nor inhibits religion."[50] It would be difficult to argue that the tax privileges do not have "a primary effect" of advancing religion.

The employment of chaplains in the armed services and prisons was defended by Justices Brennan, Goldberg and Harlan in the Schempp case, on the ground that the removal of chaplains would inhibit the free exercise of religion by those whom the government compels to be in the armed forces or prisons. Mr. Justice Clark, speaking for the Court in Schempp, admitted that there might be a denial of the free exercise of religion to those persons unless the government "permits voluntary religious services to be conducted with the use of government facilities."[51] But note that he, speaking for the Court, said nothing about chaplains, but only "government facilities." It may not be visionary to foresee this Supreme Court holding that government can permit religious services to be conducted on government property in a military or prison setting, but that there is no need, and no justification, for putting clergymen on the public payroll, except perhaps in the case of an isolated military outpost. The free exercise of religion, the Court might say, would be adequately served in the ordinary case by permitting privately-supported clergy to minister to the military personnel and prisoners on government property, including government buildings. The critical problems of tax and other financial aids to religion, including chaplains, are discussed in Chapters V and VI and on page 111.

In the long run, the school prayer decisions, if followed, predictably will have the effect of raising agnosticism to the rank of the official public religion of the United States. As will be discussed in Chapter IV, there can be no true neutrality on the part of government as between those religions that acknowledge God and those that do not. The Court now has cast aside the historical affirmation by government in this country of the essential truth of theism, has embarked upon a search for "neutrality," a search incapable of success, and has substituted agnosticism for the theistic affirmation to which a small minority has objected so strongly. And for its action the Court can point to no durable justification beyond its own inflated rhetoric and a tortured historical interpretation. In sad point of fact, the Supreme Court has now elevated itself, by its romantic reliance upon the dicta in Everson and the succeeding cases we have discussed, to a height from which there is no intellectually respectable escape except an open retreat along the path by which it ascended—a retreat to a sound historical and legal construction of the First Amendment. The alternatives are, either a maintenance of the erroneous reigning theories coupled with a less than candid refusal to apply them to the extremes which their logic commands, or a rigorous implementation of those theories to a point where the frank abrogation of our religious heritage will assume preposterous dimensions.

I

1. 370 U.S. 421 (1962).
2. 370 U.S. at 430.
3. *Abington School District v. Schempp,* 374 U.S. 203, 212 (1963).
4. 374 U.S. at 209
5. 374 U.S. 203 (1963).
6. See *Wall Street Journal,* September 5, 1963.
7. 330 U.S. 1 (1947).
8. 330 U.S. at 15–16.
9. *McCollum v. Board of Education,* 333 U.S. 203 (1948).
10. 333 U.S. at 210–211.
11. 333 U.S. at 211
12. 333 U.S. at 212.
13. 333 U.S. at 212.
14. See 233 U.S. at 231
15. *Zorach v. Clauson,* 343 U.S. 306 (1952).
16. 343 U.S. at 315.
17. 343 U.S. at 312.
18. 343 U.S. at 312–313
19. *Engel v. Vitale,* 370 U.S. 421, 437, 439, 441 (1962).
20. 343 U.S. at 313.
21. *McGowan v. Maryland,* 366 U.S. 420 (1961).
22. *Two Guys from Harrison-Allentown, Inc. v. McGinley,* 366 U.S. U.S. 582 (1961); *Braunfeld v. Brown,* 366 U.S. 599 (1961).
23. *Gallagher v. Crown Kosher Super Market,* 366 U.S. 617 (1961).
24. 366 U.S. at 443.
25. *Torcaso v. Watkins,* 367 U.S. 488 (1961).
26. 367 U.S. at 496.
27. 333 U.S. at 213, 232, quoted in the Torcaso case at 367 U.S. 493–494.
28. 370 U.S. at 435.
29. 374 U.S. at 225.
30. 374 U.S. at 222.
31. 370 U.S. at 425.

32. 370 U.S. at 431.
33. 374 U.S. at 222, 225.
34. 370 U.S. at 431.
35. 370 U.S. at 437.
36. 374 U.S. at 222.
37. *Everson v. Board of Education,* 330 U.S. 1, 15 (1947).
38. 374 U.S. at 216.
39. Dissenting opinion of Mr. Justice Jackson in *Everson v. Board of Education,* 330 U.S. 1, 26 (1947).
40. Dissenting opinion of Mr. Justice Rutledge, joined by Justice Frankfurter, Jackson and Burton, in *Everson v. Board of Education,* 330 U.S. 1, 31–32 (1947).
41. Dissenting opinion of Mr. Justice Rutledge, joined by Justices Frankfurter, Jackson and Burton, in *Everson v. Board of Education,* 330 U.S. 1, 52 (1947).
42. Concurring opinion of Mr. Justice Frankfurter, joined by Justices Jackson, Rutledge and Burton, in *McCollum v. Board of Education,* 333 U.S. 203, 227 (1948).
43. Mr. Justice Black for the Court in *Torcaso v. Watkins,* 367 U.S. 488, 495 (1961).
44. Mr. Justice Black for the Court in *Engel v. Vitale,* 370 U.S. 421, 431 (1962).
45. 374 U.S. at 222.
46. 374 U.S. at 304.
47. Report No. 1693, 83rd Cong., 2d Sess.
48. 374 U.S. at 303.
49. 370 U.S. at 435.
50. 374 U.S. at 222.
51. 374 U.S. at 226.

And have we now forgotten that powerful friend? or do we imagine that we no longer need his assistance? I have lived, Sir, a long time, and the longer I live, the more convincing proofs I see of this truth—that God governs in the affairs of men. *And if a sparrow cannot fall to the ground without his notice, is it probable that an empire can rise without his aid?*

BENJAMIN FRANKLIN
The Constitutional Convention of 1787

II

America Recognizes God: Up to 1791

COLONIAL BACKGROUND

It was not surprising that the school prayer rulings provoked a vigorous opposition. The fact is that they challenged a fundamental, though often unacknowledged, postulate of American society. Historical evidence of an impressive magnitude and variety compels the conclusion that the American colonies, the independent American states, and finally the United States of America, were all premised, in their juridical and social structure, upon the facts that there is a providential Creator and that man, society and the state ought in some way to acknowledge Him and His law. Excerpts from representative colonial charters and colonial public documents are collected in *Appendix A*. They demonstrate the existence of these premises of colonial government and show that often an expressed purpose of a colonial enterprise was such as to aid "in propagating of *Christian* Religion to such People, as yet live in Darkness and miserable Ignorance of the true Knowledge and Worship of God. . . ." (First Charter of Virginia, 1606). Significantly, when the Virginia settlers arrived at Jamestown in 1607, the first permanent building they erected was a church.

This is not to say that the colonization of America was essentially a missionary endeavor. Far from it. It had other and more remembered purposes and elements than the evangelical. But what can be said is that the colonizing effort, to a noticeable degree, was religiously motivated, either by a zeal for proselytization or a desire for refuge from persecution. And uniformly the colonies juridically acknowledged their debt to God. For instance, John Locke, the philosopher upon whose ideas the framers of the Declaration of Independence and Constitution were nourished, provided in Article 95 of the Fundamental Constitutions of Carolina of 1669, which he framed, that: "No man shall be permitted to be a freeman of Carolina, or to have any estate or habitation within it, that doth not acknowledge a God, and that God is publicly and solemnly to be worshipped."[1] It was not accidental that when the Liberty Bell was cast in 1751, a biblical inscription was chosen from the words of Moses, "Proclaim liberty throughout the land upon all the inhabitants thereof" (Lev. 25:10). The colonists apparently believed, as did William Penn, that: "Those People who are not governed by God will be ruled by tyrants."

FROM INDEPENDENCE TO 1787

The recognition by the colonists of the position and superintendence of God survived the turbulent transition from colonial status to independence. The law of God was asserted as a principal justification for the break from the Crown, and the leaders of the Revolution were explicit in praying divine assistance and exhorting the citizens to do likewise. The Continental Congress, in September, 1774, began its session with a prayer led by an Episcopal cleric[2] and, on June 12, 1775, that Congress proclaimed "a day of public humiliation, fasting and prayer; that we may, with united hearts and voices, unfeignedly confess and deplore our many sins; and offer up our joint supplications to the all-wise, omnipotent, and merciful Disposer of all events. . . ."[3] Similar days of fasting and prayer were proclaimed in the succeeding years. It may be incidental, but the Continental Congress suspended its deliberations on Good Fridays, a practice continued by the First Congress under the Constitution.

When the Continental Congress, on July 6, 1775, solemnly proclaimed its Declaration of the Causes and Necessity of Taking Up Arms, it asserted, after a reference to "the divine Author of our existence," that:

> a reverence for our great Creator, principles of humanity, and the dictates of common sense, must convince all those who reflect upon the subject, that government was instituted to promote the welfare of mankind, and ought to be administered for the attainment of that end.

And the Congress concluded the Declaration:

> With an humble confidence in the mercies of the supreme and impartial Judge and Ruler of the Universe, we most devoutly implore his divine goodness to protect us happily through this great conflict, to dispose our adversaries to reconciliation on reasonable terms, and thereby to relieve the empire from the calamities of civil war.[4]

The Declaration of Independence acknowledged God in four separate places. The framers of that instrument announced that the colonies were assuming "the separate and equal station to which the laws of nature and of nature's God entitle them." This reference to nature and nature's God was probably deistic, in that the phrase was in common use by the deists of that day, who believed in a God but did not ascribe to Him a continuing, providential concern for human affairs. The three other references to God in the Declaration, however, were frankly theistic in their recognition of God and His providence:

> We hold these truths to be self-evident: that all men are created equal; that they are endowed, by their Creator, with certain unalienable rights; that among these are life, liberty, and the pursuit of happiness.

> We, therefore, the representatives of the UNITED STATES OF AMERICA, in General Congress assembled, appealing to the Supreme Judge of the world for the rectitude of our intentions, do . . . solemnly publish and declare, That these United Colonies are, and of right ought to be, FREE and INDEPENDENT STATES. . . .

> And for the support of this Declaration, with a firm reliance on the protection of DIVINE PROVIDENCE, we mutually pledge to each other our lives, our fortunes, and our sacred honour.

Unlike the Declaration of Independence, the Constitution of the United States makes no reference to God. The only reference to religion in the Constitution, prior to the addition of the First Amendment, was the prohibition in Article VI that "no religious test shall ever be required as a qualification to any office or public trust under the United States." It ought not to be inferred, however, that the omission of God from the Constitution was a repudiation of the affirmations in the Declaration. Such an inference can be drawn only by reading the Constitution in a vacuum without regard to the historical context in which it was framed and adopted. The unbroken sequence of public acknowledgments of the Deity did not end with the Declaration of Independence. Rather they continued through the entire period here under consideration. The Constitutional Convention of 1787, and the debates in the First Congress which proposed the Bill of Rights for adoption by the states, will be considered in the next section. Suffice it here to say that, between 1776 and 1787, when the Constitution was framed, there were plentiful indications that the spiritual foundations of colonial society remained intact. For example, five days after the Declaration of Independence, General George Washington, pursuant to authorization of the Continental Congress, directed all regimental commanders to procure chaplains and to "see that all inferior officers and soldiers pay them a suitable respect and attend carefully upon religious exercises." "The blessings and protection of Heaven," the directive said, "are at all times necessary, but especially so in times of public distress and danger. The General hopes and trusts, that every officer and man will endeavor so to live and act, as becomes a Christian soldier defending the dearest Rights and Liberties of his country."[5]

Even before the Declaration of Independence, the colonists had begun to form state governments and adopt constitutions. By the spring of 1777, every colony had organized an independent government, with eleven proclaiming new constitutions, and Connecticut and Rhode Island continuing to operate under the framework of their liberal colonial charters. In all thirteen of these instruments, the new states recognized God and His preeminence. At the start of the Revolution there were established, state-supported churches in at least nine colonies. Four of these establishments were still in existence at the adoption of the Constitution of the United States.

The Continental Congress opened its sessions, beginning in 1774, with prayer delivered by a clergyman. In 1776, regular chaplains were authorized and subsequently appointed by the Congress.[6] In 1788, Congress provided an annual salary for the chaplains.[7] The Continental Congress also appointed chaplains for various military units and hospitals. During the period between independence and the framing of the Constitution, state conventions and legislatures also regularly employed and paid chaplains.

On March 1, 1781, the Continental Congress adopted the Articles of Confederation, under which the new nation was to be governed, and in them the Congress paid its respects to "the great Governor of the world." Later, in 1787, that Congress adopted the Northwest Ordinance, for the governance of the Northwest Territory. Article 3 proclaimed: "Religion, morality, and knowledge, being necessary to good government and the happiness of mankind, schools and the means of education shall forever be encouraged."[8]

The Northwest Ordinance was the foremost achievement of the Congress under the Articles of Confederation, and it was adopted while the Constitutional Convention of 1787 was in session. The Ordinance, including Article 3 with its sanction of a benevolent promotion by the state of religious education, was adopted verbatim by the First Congress on August 7, 1789, during the period when Congress was considering the proposed amendments to the Constitution, including the First Amendment. The terms of the Ordinance were later made applicable, in 1790 and 1800, to the territory south of the Ohio River and to the Indiana Territory.[9]

Many more examples could be cited to show that, from Independence to the framing of the Constitution, the public life of the American states was based upon the unapologetic conviction that there is a God who exercises a benevolent providence over the affairs of men. That is not to say that all Americans then recognized God, or that there was agreement on all details of His attributes. But to those who assert that the First Amendment was designed to prevent the government from recognizing God and praying His aid, it can rightly be said that they will have to find evidence for their claim elsewhere than in the history of the period prior to 1787. General Washington's comments to the governors of the States, upon disbanding the Continental Army in 1783, illustrates a readiness to affirm the supernatural basis of society which appears to have been characteristic of the times:

> I now make it my earnest prayer, that God would have you, and the State over which you preside, in his holy protection; that he would incline the hearts of the citizens to cultivate a spirit of subordination and obedience to government; to entertain a brotherly affection and love for one another, for their fellow citizens of the United States at large, and particularly for their brethren who have served in the field; and, finally, that he would most graciously be pleased to dispose us all to do justice, to love mercy, and to demean ourselves with that charity, humility, and pacific temper of mind, which were the characteristics of the Divine Author of our blessed religion, and without an humble imitation of whose example in these things, we can never hope to be a happy nation.[10]

At the close of the Revolution, the treaty of peace with Great Britain began: "In the name of the Most Holy and Undivided Trinity."[11]

Opponents of governmental recognition of God, including the Justices of the Supreme Court, frequently point to the *Memorial and Remonstrance* of James Madison to prove that the First Amendment, of which Madison was a leading architect, was designed to interdict such recognition. The Virginia Bill of Rights, in 1776, did not abolish the Anglican establishment in that state, but Article 16 thereof, coauthored by Madison and George Mason, proclaimed, "that religion, or the duty which we owe to our Creator, and the manner of discharging it, can be directed only by reason and conviction, not by force or violence. . . ." In the Virginia General Assembly of 1779, Thomas Jefferson introduced his Bill for Establishing Religious Freedom, designed to terminate the official Anglican establishment. When Jefferson left for Europe in 1784, Madison became the chief sponsor of the Bill until its enactment in 1786. The climax came in 1784 and

1785, with the struggle over the Assessment Bill, entitled, "A Bill for Establishing a Provision for Teachers of the Christian Religion." That bill, supported by Washington, future Chief Justice John Marshall and other outstanding Virginians, levied an assessment upon all taxpayers for the support of the Christian religion, with the taxpayer having the privilege of designating which church would receive his money and with the money, in the absence of a choice by the taxpayer, going for the support of education. It aroused fears that it would lead to a reactivation of the official preference of the Anglican Church. In the Assembly, the Assessment Bill was championed by Patrick Henry. The fiery Henry was such a fearsome opponent, before Madison induced him to leave the Assembly and become Governor, that Jefferson wrote from Paris to Madison, "What we have to do, I think, is devotedly to pray for his death."—an interesting intrusion of prayer into public affairs.[12]

Madison vehemently opposed the Assessment Bill and, in 1785, he issued his *Memorial and Remonstrance* against it. He attacked the proposal as an establishment of Christianity, and said:

> (I)t is proper to take alarm at the first experiment on our liberties. . . . Who does not see that the same authority which can establish Christianity, in exclusion of all other Religions, may establish with the same ease any particular sect of Christianity, in exclusion of all other Sects? That the same authority which can force a citizen to contribute three pence only of his property for the support of any one establishment, may force him to conform to any other establishment in all cases whatsoever?

Madison also declared in the *Memorial and Remonstrance* that "religion is wholly exempt" from the "cognizance" of civil society. The *Remonstrance* generated a flood of petitions to the General Assembly, contributing to the final defeat in committee of the Assessment Bill in December, 1785. Madison then achieved the passage, in January, 1786, of Jefferson's long-pending Bill for Establishing Religious Freedom, terminating the official preference of the Anglican Church.

Madison's *Remonstrance* has frequently been recognized

by the Supreme Court as an important guide for determining the meaning of the First Amendment, which he helped to draft. Certainly, the significance of the *Remonstrance* ought not to be minimized. On the other hand, it will not bear the broad interpretations which have been laid upon it, especially in the current controversy. In the school prayer dispute, the relevant question concerning the *Remonstrance* is whether it was intended to prohibit prayer to God by the government of Virginia. Such an intention cannot be found in that paper. The *Remonstrance* was directed against a preferential law channeling tax funds directly and solely to the support of a favored religion, that is, the Christian church of the taxpayers' choice or, if the taxpayer made no choice, then to the support of education. Such a law would properly run afoul of the restrictions of the First Amendment today. But the *Remonstance,* as a challenge to that preferential law, cannot be construed to imply that Madison then objected to governmental recognition of the Deity. Indeed, Madison ended the *Remonstrance* itself with a prayer:

> We the subscribers say that the General Assembly of this Commonwealth have no such authority: And that no effort may be omitted on our part against so dangerous an usurpation, we oppose to it, this remonstrance; earnestly praying, as we are in duty bound, that the Supreme Lawgiver of the Universe, by illuminating those to whom it is addressed, may on the one hand, turn their councils from every act which would affront his holy prerogative, or violate the trust committed to them: and on the other, guide them into every measure which may be worthy of his blessing, may redound to their own praise, and establish more firmly the liberties, the prosperity, and the Happiness of the Commonwealth.[13]

It should also be noted that James Madison was not alone the author of the First Amendment, though his important role in its construction cannot be denied. Even if the *Remonstrance* could be interpreted as inimical to all governmental promotion of prayer, that interpretation would not foreclose discussion of the meaning of the First Amendment. The fact, of course, is that it cannot be so interpreted. It probably would advance understanding if some opponents of government-sponsored prayer would cease their uncritical and somewhat mystical invocation of Madison and his *Remonstrance.*

THE CONSTITUTIONAL CONVENTION

> "Let us raise a standard to which the wise and honest can repair; the event is in the hand of God." George Washington, President of the Constitutional Convention of 1787.

The Constitutional Convention began its deliberations on May 25, 1787. Its sessions continued through the summer and the Constitution was signed on the following September 17th. Except for the previously noted prohibition against religious tests for public office, the Constitution mentions neither God nor religion. In fact, but for the religious test matter and an unsuccessful attempt by Benjamin Franklin to introduce a prayer into the proceedings, religion did not enter into the Convention debates.

There are several possible explanations for this omission. One is that most of the colonies had only recently thrown off the established Anglican or Congregational churches, and so the delegates may have been reluctant to intrude the subject of religion into the deliberations for fear that the discussion might lead to some form of federal establishment. Or, they may have felt that it would have introduced a needless, divisive element into the already complex deliberations. For either reason, the members of the Convention may have concluded that it would be better to leave the establishment problem entirely to the states. Indeed, the prohibition in Article VI of religious tests for public office was an indirect method of preventing a federal established church, since the test oath historically had been a chief instrument for excluding from office all who would not conform to an established church.

It is sometimes asserted that the absence of any religious provision in the Constitution betokened an attitude of hostility toward religion on the part of the Convention. At least, it is said, the framers intended the federal government to be neutral on all questions of God, including the question of His very existence. Such conclusions are tenable only by abstracting the debates from their historical setting. It must be remembered that the basic question today is whether the founding fathers intended to prohibit the federal government from sponsoring the recognition and invocation of God as a part of public events. The answer to this question is clearly negative. One reason for the answer is that while the Constitution was the blueprint establishing the framework of the government of the United States, the philosophical underpinning for that framework must be sought elsewhere. The Constitution was, in a sense, a technical work. Its philosophical tone was set, not in itself, but in the Declaration of Independence. There we find the recognition of unalienable, God-given rights, and the basic affirmation: "That to secure these rights, governments are instituted among men . . . ." There we find also the frank and unashamed recognition of the role of God. The disposition to acknowledge God and his providence in public affairs continued after the Declaration up to the very time of the Constitutional Convention. As we shall see, it has continued thereafter, at least until 1962.

It would require more than mere silence on the part of the 1787 Convention to imply a rejection of the previously conceded and continuous function of government as a promoter of the recognition of God. It is improbable that the otherwise unbroken history of such governmental activity was interrupted only for the four months that the framers deliberated, and that their deliberations were premised upon an antagonism to that activity and resulted in a prohibition of it forevermore. If that were the disposition of the Convention, would it not have provoked objection from some of the members? But there was no objection. The general concurrence of the membership in the omission of religion from the debates is more reasonably ascribed to a desire to avoid stirring a hornet's nest on a subject which they thought would be better left to the states anyway. A desire of this sort is fully consistent with a benevolent attitude toward religion in general and governmental recognition of the existence of God.

The failure of the attempt by Benjamin Franklin to introduce prayer into the proceedings in no way detracts from this conclusion. In the course of their deliberations, the delegates reached an impasse on the questions of the method of apportionment of Congressional representation among the States and the extent to which the States would relinquish their sovereignty. At a critical juncture, on Thursday, June 28, 1787, Benjamin Franklin rose and moved that the Convention resort to prayer in its search for a resolution of its difficulties. The fact that his motion was not carried has been used by some to imply a hostility on the part of the Convention to governmentally-sponsored prayer. The facts will not support that interpretation as will be seen from James Madison's report of the incident as contained in his notes on the Convention. Mr. Franklin rose to suggest:

> Mr. President
> The small progress we have made after 4 or five weeks close attendance & continual reasonings with each other—our different sentiments on almost every question, several of the last producing as many noes as ays, is methinks a melancholy proof of the imperfection of the Human Understanding. We indeed seem to feel our own want of political wisdom, since we have been running about in search of it. We have gone back to ancient history for models of Government, and examined the different forms of those Republics which having been formed with the seeds of their own dissolution now no longer exist. And we have viewed Modern States all round Europe, but find none of their Constitutions suitable to our circumstances.
> In this situation of this Assembly, groping as it were in the dark to find political truth, and scarce able to distinguish it when presented to us, how has it happened, Sir, that we have not hitherto once thought of humbly applying to the Father of lights to illuminate our understandings? In the beginning of the Contest with G. Britain, when we were sensible of danger we had daily prayer in this room for the divine protection.—Our prayers, Sir, were heard, & they were graciously answered. All of us who were engaged in the struggle must have observed frequent instances of a superintending providence in our favor. To that kind providence we owe this happy opportunity of consulting in peace on the means of establishing our future national felicity. And have we now forgotten that powerful friend? or do we imagine that we no longer need his assistance? I have lived, Sir, a long time, and the longer I live, the more convincing proofs I see of this truth—*that God governs in the affairs of men.* And if a sparrow cannot fall to the

ground without his notice, is it probable that an empire can rise without his aid? We have been assured, Sir, in the sacred writings, that "except the Lord build the House they labour in vain that build it." I firmly believe this; and I also believe that without his concurring aid we shall succeed in this political building no better, than the Builders of Babel: We shall be divided by our little partial local interests; our projects will be confounded, and we ourselves shall become a reproach and bye word down to future ages. And what is worse, mankind may hereafter from this unfortunate instance, despair of establishing Governments by Human wisdom and leave it to chance, war and conquest.

I therefore beg leave to move—that henceforth prayers imploring the assistance of Heaven, and its blessings on our deliberations, be held in this Assembly every morning before we proceed to business, and that one or more of the Clergy of this City be requested to officiate in that Service—

Mr. Madison's notes continue:

Mr. SHARMAN[14] seconded the motion.

Mr. HAMILTON & several others expressed their apprehensions that however proper such a resolution might have been at the beginning of the convention, it might at this late day, 1. bring on it some disagreeable animadversions. & 2. lead the public to believe that the embarrassments and dissensions within the Convention, had suggested this measure. It was answered by Docr. F. Mr. SHERMAN & others, that the past omission of a duty could not justify a further omission—that the rejection of such a proposition would expose the Convention to more unpleasant animadversions than the adoption of it: and that the alarm out of doors that might be excited for the state of things within, would at least be as likely to do good as ill.

Mr. WILLIAMSON, observed that the true cause of the omission could not be mistaken. The Convention had no funds.

Mr. RANDOLPH proposed in order to give a favorable aspect to ye measure, that a sermon be preached at the request of the convention on 4th of July, the anniversary of Independence; & thenceforward prayers be used in ye Convention every morning. Dr. Frankn 2ded this motion After several unsuccessful attempts for silently postponing the matter by ad-

> journg the adjournment was at length carried, without any vote on the motion.[15]

Rather than indicating an aversion of the delegates to public prayer, the Madison report of the incident shows their reluctance was prompted by fear of alarming the populace through a sudden resort to prayer which could indicate that the Convention was in serious difficulty. The remark of Mr. Hugh Williamson of North Carolina implies that the real reason for the omission of prayer may have been simply the lack of funds to pay a chaplain. In any event, there is no evidence in this episode that the founding fathers felt public prayer as such to be beyond the reach of their power or function. The lack of any such assertion by any delegate at the time justifies the conclusion that they had few, if any, qualms about public prayer in general, and would not have hesitated to employ it had it been suggested at a time when the action would not have been subject to misconstruction.

THE FIRST CONGRESS

The Constitution was approved by the Federal Convention on September 17, 1787. It became binding among the states that had ratified it on June 21, 1788, when New Hampshire became the ninth state to ratify. Congress ordered the Constitution to be put into operation on September 13, 1788.

Various amendments were formally proposed by seven state-ratifying conventions. Of these, five states proposed amendments or declarations to ensure religious liberty. Virginia's was typical of four of them and provided:

> That religion or the duty which we owe to our Creator, and the manner of discharging it can be directed only by reason and conviction, not by force or violence, and therefore all men have an equal, natural and unalienable right to the free exercise of religion according to the dictates of conscience, and that no particular religious sect or society ought to be favored or established by Law in preference to others.[16]

New Hampshire's proposed amendment was broader: "Congress shall make no Laws touching Religion, or to infringe the rights of Conscience."[17] But this broad language of New Hampshire, which was later considered and rejected by the

First Congress, did not imply that the federal government ought to be powerless even to recognize God. In fact, the New Hampshire Convention included in that same ratifying resolution an expression of gratitude to "the Supreme Ruler of the Universe" for the favor of "his Providence."

Acting upon the proposals, the Congress submitted twelve amendments to the legislatures of the states on September 25, 1789. The first two, relating to apportionment of the House of Representatives and requiring the intervention of an election of Representatives before any variance in the compensation of Senators and Representatives could go into effect, failed of ratification. The last ten of the twelve amendments submitted to the states were adopted and became effective in December of 1791. They are known, of course, as the Bill of Rights.

The first two clauses of the First Amendment, as adopted by the states, read: "Congress shall make no law respecting an establishment of religion, or prohibiting the free exercise thereof." To fathom the meaning of these provisions, it would be wise to follow the suggestion of Thomas Jefferson, who wrote in a letter to William Johnson in 1823:

> On every question of construction, carry ourselves back to the time when the Constitution was adopted, recollect the spirit manifested in the debates, and instead of trying what meaning may be squeezed out of the text, or invented against it, conform to the probable one in which it was passed.[18]

Seen in this light, the First Amendment cannot realistically be construed to foreclose all official recognition of God and His providence, and all governmentally sponsored prayer. The First Congress, which proposed the Amendment, was surely not hostile to such prayer. For example, both Houses of the First Congress appointed chaplains at the outset of their first session. In 1788, these chaplains were put on the federal payroll. The practice of Congress in employing chaplains for both houses has continued to the present time. The First Congress also appointed chaplains for military units. It was moved in the Senate that there should be a religious service, in a church no less, as part of President Washington's first inauguration:

> Resolved, that after the oath shall have been administered to the President, he, attended by the Vice President, and members of the Senate and House of Representatives, proceed to St. Paul's Chapel, to hear divine service, to be performed by the Chaplain of Congress already appointed.[19]

The measure passed both Houses practically unchanged. The service in St. Paul's Chapel was an Anglican service, including the *Te Deum,* and was performed by the Rt. Rev. Samuel Provoost, Episcopal Bishop of New York and Chaplain of the Senate.[20] In view of this, what becomes of the argument advanced in some quarters today that the First Amendment, proposed by that same Congress, prohibits prayers offered or sponsored by government officials?

President Washington initiated a custom which has been followed by every President to the present day when he inserted a prayerful reference to God in his inaugural address:

> It would be peculiarly improper to omit in this first official act my fervent supplication to that almighty Being who rules over the universe, who presides in the councils of nations and whose providential aids can supply every human defect, that His benediction may consecrate to the liberties and happiness of the people of the United States a government instituted by themselves for these essential purposes. . . .

President Washington inaugurated another custom which has continued unbroken when he added the words, "So help me God," to the constitutional oath of office. Most Presidents since have also placed a hand on the Bible while reciting the oath. (President Lincoln is reported to have kissed the Bible at his inauguration.) There is no indication of opposition by the First Congress to those actions of the first President. The religious elements which he and the Congress freely included in his inauguration help us to understand Washington's explanation, in a letter written later in 1789 to the New England Presbyterian churches, of the lack of religious references in the Constitution itself:

> And here I am persuaded, you will permit me to observe, that *the path of true piety is so plain, as to require but little POLITICAL direction.*
>
> *To this consideration we ought to ascribe the absence of any regulation respecting religion from the Magna Charta of our*

> *country.* To the guidance of the Ministers of the Gospel, this important object is, perhaps, more properly committed. It will be your care to instruct the ignorant, and to reclaim the devious: And in the progress of morality and science, to which our Government will give every furtherance, we may confidently expect the advancement of true religion, and the completion of our happiness." (Italics in original.)[21]

Washington surely did not believe that the constitutional prohibition against the establishment of a favored sect disabled the government even from recognizing God and imploring His aid.

In view of this historical setting, it is at least implausible to assert that the absence of religious reference in the Constitution as originally adopted implies that the Constitutional Convention, over which Washington presided, and the First Congress intended to disable the federal government from all public official recognition and supplication of God.

Moreover, the debates in the First Congress on the proposed amendment indicate clearly the limited scope its framers intended the First Amendment to have. On April 8, 1789, James Madison introduced in the House of Representatives the original proposal leading to the First Amendment. It read:

> The civil rights of none shall be abridged on account of religious belief or worship, nor shall any national religion be established, nor shall the full and equal rights of conscience be in any manner, or on any pretext, infringed.[22]

When, on August 15, 1789, the House resolved itself into a committee of the whole to consider this proposition, Representative Elbridge Gerry of Massachusetts "said it would read better if it was, that no religious doctrine shall be established by law."[23] The Annals record that: "MR. MADISON said, he apprehended the meaning of the words to be, that Congress should not establish a religion, and enforce the legal observation of it by law, nor compel men to worship God in any manner contrary to their conscience."[24] Mr. Benjamin Huntington of Connecticut then expressed a far-sighted apprehension as to the way in which the amendment could be misconstrued to permit overscrupulous exclusion of religious groups from receipt of benefits available to the general citizenry, for example, the enforcement in federal courts of civil contracts relating to church affairs:

> MR. HUNTINGTON said that he feared, with the gentleman (Mr. Silvester of New York) first up on this subject, that the words might be taken in such latitude as to be extremely hurtful to the cause of religion. He understood the amendment to mean what had been expressed by the gentleman from Virginia; but others might find it convenient to put another construction upon it. The ministers of their congregations to the Eastward were maintained by the contributions of those who belonged to their society; the expense of building meeting-houses was contributed in the same manner. These things were regulated by by-laws. If an action was brought before a Federal Court on any of these cases, the person who had neglected to perform his engagements could not be compelled to do it; for a support of ministers or building of places of worship might be construed into a religious establishment.
>
> By the charter of Rhode Island, no religion could be established by law; he could give a history of the effects of such a regulation; indeed the people were now enjoying the blessed fruits of it. He hoped, therefore, the amendment would be made in such a way as to secure the rights of conscience, and a free exercise of the rights of religion, *but not to patronise those who professed no religion at all* (Italics added).[25]

His reference to the absence of an established religion in Rhode Island shows that Huntington, and presumably the other members of the Congress, understood establishment to mean the official preference of a single sect, since the Rhode Island charter proclaimed as the reason for its guarantee of religious freedom the fact that some of the colonists could not in conscience conform to "the liturgy, formes and ceremonyes of the Church of England."

It would be interesting to have Mr. Huntington's unvarnished opinion of the Engel, Murray and Schempp decisions. Huntington was obviously opposed to a construction of the amendment which would patronize atheists or agnostics, and no other member of the Congress disputed the point. Mr. Madison did comment by stating his understanding of the limited scope of the amendment:

> MR. MADISON thought, if the word *"national"* was inserted before religion, it would satisfy the minds of honorable gentlemen. He believed that *the people feared one sect might obtain a pre-eminence, or two combine together, and establish a religion to which they would compel others to conform.* He thought if the word "national" was introduced, it would point the amendment directly to the object it was intended to prevent (Italics added).[26]

Ultimately, the word "national" was left out of the amendment. That its exclusion turned upon reasons of federal-state relations, and not upon religious causes, was made clear by Mr. Gerry in the debate:

> MR. GERRY did not like the term national, proposed by the gentleman from Virginia, and he hoped it would not be adopted by the House. It brought to his mind some observations that had taken place in the conventions at the time they were considering the present Constitution. It had been insisted upon by those who were called anti-federalists, that this form of Government consolidated the Union; the honorable gentleman's motion shows that he considers it in the same light. Those who were called anti-federalists at that time, complained that they had injustice done them by the title, because they were in favor of a Federal Government, and the others were in favor of a national one. . . .[27]

Mr. Madison then withdrew his motion to insert the word "national" before "religion." The House, on August 20, 1789, approved the following language: "Congress shall make no law establishing religion, or to prevent the free exercise thereof, or to infringe the rights of conscience."[28] The Senate approved a version reading: "Congress shall make no law establishing articles of faith or a mode of worship or prohibiting the free exercise of religion."[29]

The Senate-House conference worked out the final version of the amendment as it ultimately was approved by the States. (There was practically no discussion of the religion amendment in the State Legislatures which ratified the Bill of Rights).

Professor Edward S. Corwin explains Congress' intention:

> That is, Congress shall not prescribe a national faith, a possibility which those states with establishments of their own

> . . . probably regarded with fully as much concern as those which had gotten rid of their establishments.[30]

Throughout the debates in the House and Senate, and in the language of the several versions proposed, there was not the slightest indication that the designers of the amendment aimed at prohibiting all governmentally-sponsored prayer and acknowledgment of God. Surely such an attitude cannot be discerned in the conduct of James Madison during the proceedings. Madison, it should be recalled, served agreeably on the committee which selected chaplains for the House and Senate. He supported the bill for chaplains in the armed services. Later he was to approve, as President, bills appropriating funds for the salaries of chaplains in Congress and in the armed services and for the promotion of religious education among certain Indian tribes. He was personally a quite religious man, as shown by his expressions in a letter in 1825.:

> And the belief in a God All Powerful wise and good, is so essential to the moral order of the World and to the happiness of man, that arguments which enforce it cannot be drawn from too many sources nor adapted with too much solicitude to the different characters and capacities to be impressed with it.[31]

Mr. Madison apparently conceived the establishment clause of the Amendment to be directed against the same evil which was the target of his *Memorial and Remonstrance*—the establishment of a particular sect or combination of sects as a direct and favored beneficiary of public funds. At least, that clearly was his attitude at the time of the events.

We are told today, however, that any law permitting governmental recognition of God is a law respecting an establishment of theistic religion, to the exclusion of religions that do not acknowledge God. Thereby, we are told, the First Amendment is infringed because the mere supplication of God by government is the sort of establishment which the First Congress, and especially Madison, sought to forestall. The truth of the matter is quite the contrary. The prior history and the debates in the First Congress, as we have seen, show that Congress desired to prevent the extension of official federal favor to any one or exclusive combination of sects acknowledging God. The established church in England, which the founding fathers sought to prevent in the United States, had been characterized by public subsidy of its clergy alone, the extension of the right to vote and hold public office to its members alone, and similar emoluments of a favored position. This preferential treatment of one or a combination of Christian sects, as an instrument of royal power, was the evil against which the establishment clause was directed. By the exclusion of sectarian favoritism the free exercise of religion by all would be promoted. Madison's comments in the debate indicate that this was his purpose, too. In case there is any doubt as to Madison's concept of the word "establishment," an extract from one of his later letters should settle the point:

> It was the belief of all sects at one time that the establishment of Religion by law was right and necessary; that the true religion ought to be established in exclusion of every other; and that the only question to be decided was, what was the true religion. The example of Holland proved that a toleration of sects dissenting from the established sect was safe, and even useful. The example of the Colonies, now States, which rejected religious establishments altogether, proved that all sects might be safely and advantageously put on a footing of equal and entire freedom. . . .[32]

In the Virginia Convention in 1788, which ratified the Constitution of the United States, and only one year before he introduced his proposed religious liberty amendment in the First Congress, Madison evidenced the same opinion:

> Fortunately for this Commonwealth, a majority of the people are decidedly against any exclusive establishment. . . . A particular state might concur in one religious project. But the United States abound in such a variety of sects, that it is a strong security against religious persecution, and it is sufficient to authorize a conclusion, that no one sect will ever be able to outnumber or depress the rest.[33]

It is clear that Madison then considered an establishment of religion to mean the preferential treatment by government of one or a few of the many religious sects. He did not then consider it to include the mere recognition by government of God's existence, although he much later had some reservations on that score, which will be discussed on page 64.

As Judge Thomas Cooley, a leading constitutional scholar of the nineteenth century, put it:

> By establishment of religion is meant the setting up or recognition of a state church, or at least the conferring upon one church of special favors and advantages which are denied to others. It was never intended by the Constitution that the government should be prohibited from recognizing religion, or that religious worship should never be provided for in cases where a proper recognition of Divine Providence in the working of government might seem to require it, and where it might be done without drawing any invidious distinctions between different religious beliefs, organizations, or sects. The Christian religion was always recognized in the administration of the common law; and so far as that law continues to be the law of the land, the fundamental principles of that religion must continue to be recognized in the same cases and to the same extent as formerly.[34]

In summary, the Constitution, and the First Amendment to it, were part of, and not alien to, the stream of American thought and tradition. An important part of that tradition was expressed in the religious affirmations in the Declaration of Independence. The Constitution and Bill of Rights made operative the principles of that Declaration. There is no evidence that the Constitution and Bill of Rights disabled the federal government from affirming as true what had been categorically asserted a few years before in the document by which this nation was created. Nor could it have been otherwise. John Adams, who presided over the Senate when it considered the First Amendment, said in 1798, "Our Constitution was made only for a moral and religious people. It is wholly inadequate to the government of any other."[35]

Mr. Justice Joseph Story, who served on the Supreme Court of the United States from 1811 to 1845, and who was a leading Unitarian, confirmed the plain historical meaning of the First Amendment:

> Probably at the time of the adoption of the constitution, and of the first amendment to it . . . , the general if not the universal sentiment in America was, that Christianity ought to

> receive encouragement from the state so far as was not incompatible with the private rights of conscience and the freedom of religious worship. An attempt to level all religions, and to make it a matter of state policy to hold all in utter indifference, would have created universal disapprobation, if not universal indignation.
>
> But the duty of supporting religion, and especially the Christian religion, is very different from the right to force the consciences of other men or to punish them for worshipping God in the manner which they believe their accountability to him requires. . . . The rights of conscience are, indeed, beyond the just reach of any human power. They are given by God, and cannot be encroached upon by human authority without a criminal disobedience of the precepts of natural as well as of revealed religion.
>
> The real object of the amendment was not to countenance, much less to advance, Mahometanism, or Judaism, or infidelity, by prostrating Christianity; but to exclude all rivalry among Christian sects, and to prevent any national ecclesiastical establishment which should give to a hierarchy the exclusive patronage of the national government.[36]

Even if the historical record were otherwise blank, the claim that the First Amendment was intended to bar the federal government from officially sanctioning public prayer, would be defeated by the fact that, on September 24, 1789, the very same day that it approved the First Amendment, Congress called upon the President to proclaim a national day of thanksgiving and prayer, in the following resolution:

> That a joint committee of both Houses be directed to wait upon the President of the United States to request that he would recommend to the people of the United States a day of public thanksgiving and prayer, to be observed by acknowledging, with grateful hearts, the many signal favors of Almighty God, especially by affording them an opportunity peaceably to establish a Constitution of government for their safety and happiness.[37]

President Washington issued the thanksgiving proclamation on October 3, 1789, and every President, excepting only Thomas Jefferson and Andrew Jackson, has followed suit.

Would it not have been extraordinary for Congress to request a public day of prayer, to be observed by "the people of the United States" and, on the very same day, to propose a constitutional amendment to prohibit that very type of prayer? Indeed, the specific religious issue was raised—by Representative Thomas Tucker, of South Carolina—in the debate preceding the adoption of the resolution. Mr. Tucker objected that calling upon the President to proclaim a day of prayer "is a business with which Congress have nothing to do; it is a religious matter, and, as such, is proscribed to us."[38] Congress, however, passed the resolution. If the question of Congress' competence in religious matters had not been raised, it could possibly be said that it had never occurred to the members and therefore the action of Congress ought not to be conclusive on the point. When, however, the issue was squarely joined, the First Congress deliberately overrode the same objections we hear so often today, and voted to offer public prayer to God.

Factual judgments are usually matters of probability. But it does sometimes occur that the likelihood of one solution becomes so strong as to amount to a moral certainty. If that point of certitude has not been reached on the question of the intention of the founding fathers to prohibit, or not, all public prayer, one can hardly conceive of any question, aside from the purely mathematical, where the mind could reach a morally certain answer and come to rest. The extreme anti-prayer argument drawn from the supposed intentions of the framers is against the convincing weight of the evidence.

II

1. *The Federal and State Constitutions, Colonial Charters and Other Organic Laws,* Thorpe ed., 2783 (Washington, D.C., 1909).
2. Journals of the Continental Congress, I, 27.
3. Journals of the Continental Congress, II, 87.
4. Perry, *Sources of Our Liberties* (New York, 1959), 295–300.
5. *Writings of Washington,* Fitzpatrick, ed. (1932) V, 245.
6. Journals of the Continental Congress, VI, 1033.
7. Journals of the Continental Congress, XXXIV, 71.
8. 1 Statutes of the United States, 52.
9. 1 Statutes 123; 2 Statutes, 58–59.
10. *Writings,* Sparks, ed. (1847), VIII, 452.

11. Definitive Treaty of Peace Between the United States of America and his Britannic Majesty, September 3, 1783, 8 Statutes 80.
12. See Corwin, "The Supreme Court as National School Board," 14 *Law & Contemp. Prob.* 3, 12 (1949).
13. *The Writings of James Madison,* Hunt, ed. (1901–1910), II, 183–191.
14. This is apparently a misspelling of the name of Mr. Roger Sherman of Connecticut.
15. *United States, Formation of the Union* (Government Printing Office, Washington, D.C., 1927), pp. 295–297.
16. *Ibid.* at 1030–1031.
17. *Ibid.* at 1026.
18. Ford, *The Writings of Thomas Jefferson,* X, 231 (1899).
19. Debates and Proceedings in the Congress of the United States, I, 25.
20. Freeman, Douglas Southall, George Washington (1954) VI, 196–97.
21. Stokes, *Church and State in the United States* (1950), I, 537.
22. Annals of Congress, I, 434.
23. *Ibid.* at 730.
24. *Ibid.*
25. Annals of Congress, I, 730–731.
26. Annals of Congress, I, 731.
27. *Ibid.*
28. Annals of Congress, I, 796.
29. Senate Journal for the First Session of the First Congress of the United States (New York, 1789), 117.
30. Corwin, "The Supreme Court as National School Board," 14 *Law & Contemp. Prob.* 3, 11–12 (1949).
31. Letter to Frederick Beasley, Nov. 20, 1825; Cousins, *In God We Trust* (1958) 321.
32. Letter of July 10, 1822, to Edward Livingston, *Letters and Other Writings* (New York, 1884) III, 275–276.
33. Cousins, *In God We Trust* (1958), 314–15.
34. Cooley, *Principles of Constitutional Law* (Boston, 1898), 224–25.
35. See discussion by Senator A. Willis Robertson in Report, Prayers in Public Schools and Other Matters, Senate Committee on the Judiciary (87th Cong., 2nd Sess.), 1962, 32.
36. Story, Commentaries on the Constitution of the United States (1891), Secs. 1874, 1876, 1877.
37. Annals of Congress, I, 949.
38. Annals of Congress, I, 950.

[The framers of the First Amendment] did not intend to prohibit a just expression of religious devotion by the legislators of the nation, even in their public character as legislators; . . . they did not intend to spread over all the public authorities and the whole public action of the nation the dead and revolting spectacle of atheistical apathy. . . .

COMMITTEE ON THE JUDICIARY
United States Senate (1853)

III

America Recognizes God: Since 1791

IN LEGISLATION AND STATE CONSTITUTIONS

From the adoption of the First Amendment, in 1791, to the present day, the existence and supremacy of God have been repeatedly recognized in legislation, judicial pronouncements and statements by leading Americans. It is evident, moreover, that the repeated acknowledgments of God by public authorities and civic leaders reflect a continuing consensus of the American people themselves.

In 1853, the Senate Committee on the Judiciary rejected a challenge to the employment of chaplains in Congress and the armed forces, and ruled that the practice did not violate the First Amendment, in which opinion the House Committee on the Judiciary concurred the following year. The Senators concluded:

> They (the Framers) intended, by this amendment, to prohibit "an establishment of religion" such as the English church presented, or any thing like it. But they had no fear or jealousy of religion itself, nor did they wish to see us an irreligious people; they did not intend to prohibit a just expression of religious devotion by the legislators of the nation, even in their public character as legislators; they did not intend to send our armies and navies forth to do battle for their country without any national recognition of that God on whom success or failure depends; they did not intend to spread over all the public authorities and the whole public action of the nation the dead and revolting spectacle

> of atheistical apathy. Not so had the battles of the Revolution been fought, and the deliberations of the revolutionary Congress conducted. On the contrary, all had been done with a continual appeal to the Supreme Ruler of the world, and an habitual reliance upon His protection of the righteous cause which they commended to His care.[1]

Both Houses of the Congress of the United States have continuously employed chaplains and, under their rules, every day's session is opened with a prayer. Chaplains hold commissions in all of the armed forces. Attendance at chapel services is compulsory at West Point, Annapolis and the Air Force Academy. The oaths of office taken upon enlistment or upon commissioning as an officer in the armed forces conclude with the words, "So help me God."

In 1952, Congress called upon the President to proclaim annually a National Day of Prayer. Each year the President has obliged. President Kennedy's proclamation in 1962 is significant because of its similarity to the Regents' Prayer which the Supreme Court had recently barred from the public schools. The Regents' Prayer read:

> Almighty God, we acknowledge our dependence upon Thee, and we beg thy blessings upon us, our parents, our teachers and our country.

President Kennedy said:

> WHEREAS faith in Almighty God was a dominant power in the lives of our Founding Fathers; and
> WHEREAS they expressed this faith in prayer . . . and
> WHEREAS in full recognition of our dependence upon Almighty God and for our continuing need of His great blessings, the Congress . . . approved . . . a provision that "The President shall set aside . . . a National Day of Prayer . . .:
> NOW THEREFORE. . . .
> . . . May we especially ask God's blessing upon—
> Our homes . . .;
> Our Citizens . . .;
> Our Nation . . .;
> And our world. . . ."

This recalls Justice Potter Stewart's question in his dissenting opinion in the Regents' Prayer case: " . . . is the Court suggesting that the Constitution permits judges and Congressmen and Presidents to join in prayer, but prohibits school children from doing so?"

President Kennedy proclaimed a similar day of prayer in October, 1963. Congress, in 1954, inserted the words "under God" in the pledge of allegiance. In 1956, Congress declared the national motto to be, "In God we Trust." Most of our currency bears the same motto. Since 1931, the official national anthem has been the "Star Spangled Banner," the final stanza of which proclaims:

> Blest with victory and peace, may the heav'n rescued land
> Praise the Pow'r that hath made and preserved us a nation!
> Then conquer we must, when our cause it is just;
> And this be our motto: "In God is our trust."

Every one of the fifty state constitutions contains an acknowledgment of God as the author of our liberties. Extracts from the constitutions are contained in *Appendix B*. Significantly, nearly all state constitutions also specifically prohibit in some degree the use of public funds, or at least public school money, for sectarian purposes. This correlation is important because it is sometimes wrongly inferred that advocacy of public recognition of God must logically be accompanied by advocacy of untrammeled public financial assistance to frankly sectarian enterprises. The state constitutions show that a readiness to recognize God officially is quite compatible with a disinclination to extend public financial support to sectarian institutions. As we shall see in Chapter V, the power of the state and federal governments to confer a financial benefit upon sectarian institutions is tightly circumscribed by constitutional standards requiring a public, non-sectarian purpose for the grant, compliance with equal protection and free religious exercise criteria, and other safeguards. In any event, neither the restricted nature of the constitutional power to aid sectarian religion, nor the tendency of state constitutions to invalidate all or some types of such aid, warrants the invalidation of governmental recognition of God through public prayer. For example, a survey published in 1961 revealed that some type of homeroom devotional exercises were then held in over 50 percent of the nation's public school systems and Bible reading in over 41 percent.[2] And, of course, state authorities have continually proclaimed days of prayer, fast and thanksgiving, and have included prayer as part of many public functions.

An indirect legislative acknowledgment that government may constitutionally recognize God and His supremacy is found in the history of the so-called Blaine Amendment. First introduced in Congress in 1875, and twenty times thereafter between 1876 and 1929,[3] the proposed Blaine Amendment never gained the approval of Congress and therefore was never referred for ratification to the states. It would have specifically made the states subject to the full restrictions of the religion clauses of the First Amendment, it would have expressly barred federal and state financial support of any religious "school, educational or other institution," and it would have specified that no "particular creed or tenets" of any religious denomination shall be taught in any institution supported by federal or state funds.[4] Significantly for our purpose, it would thus have barred denominational teaching in government or government-supported institutions. The repeated proposals of the amendment by that era's most militant advocates of separation of church and state indicate clearly that they considered that without the amendment such teaching would be constitutional. If so, and if the proponents of the Blaine Amendment were correct in that judgment, then the Supreme Court of today is wrong in its interpretations. For denominational teaching in public institutions is more vulnerable to constitutional attack than is devotional Bible Reading, the Lord's Prayer or non-sectarian invocations of God. If outright denominational teaching is constitutional, as the sponsors of the Blaine Amendment believed it to be (for they wanted an amendment to make it unconstitutional), then those lesser forms of recognition of God are even more so. Moreover, even the Blaine Amendment, as it was submitted to the Senate in 1875, specified that "This article shall not be construed to prohibit the reading of the Bible in any school or institution. . . ."[5] And it was, of course, conceded by its sponsors that it did not bar non-denominational invocations of God, such as are made at the opening of the Congress' daily business.[6]

RECOGNITION BY THE COURTS

Chancellor James Kent, Chief Justice of the Supreme Court of New York and one of the leading jurists in our history, observed in an 1811 opinion sustaining a conviction for blasphemy, that: "The people of this state, in common with the people of this country, profess the general doctrines of christianity, as the rule of their faith and practice. . . ."[7]

In 1844, the Supreme Court of the United States upheld the will of Stephen Girard, who bequeathed money to establish a school for orphans. His will prohibited ministers of any sect from teaching in or even visiting the school, and limited the curriculum to instruction in pure morality, general benevolence, and a love of truth, sobriety and industry, thereby excluding by implication any instruction in religion. The Court upheld the will because it was not irreconcilably hostile to Christianity. The Court observed:

> It is also said, and truly, that the Christian religion is a part of the common law of Pennsylvania. But this proposition is to be received with its appropriate qualifications, and in connection with the bill of rights of that state, as found in its constitution of government. . . . So that we are compelled to admit that although Christianity be a part of the common law of the state, yet it is so in this qualified sense, that its divine origin and truth are admitted, and therefore it is not to be maliciously and openly reviled and blasphemed against, to the annoyance of believers or the injury of the public. . . .[8]

In order for the bequest to fail, said the Court, "There must be plain, positive, and express provisions, demonstrating not only that Christianity is not to be taught; but that it is to be impugned or repudiated."[9]

In the case of *Holy Trinity Church v. United States,*[10] the Supreme Court unanimously held that a Congressional statute prohibiting the immigration of persons under contract to perform labor, did not apply to an English minister who entered this country under contract to preach at a New York church. The Court recited the legislative history of the act and then said:

> But beyond all these matters no purpose of action against religion can be imputed to any legislation, state or national,

> because this is a religious people. This is historically true. From the discovery of this continent to the present hour, there is a single voice making this affirmation. . . .[11]

After quoting extracts, religious in tone, from American historical documents, Mr. Justice Brewer, speaking for the Court, continued:

> There is no dissonance in these declarations. There is a universal language pervading them all, having one meaning; they affirm and reaffirm that this is a religious nation. These are not individual sayings, declarations of private persons; they are organic utterances; they speak the voice of the entire people. While because of a general recognition of this truth the question has seldom been presented to the courts, yet we find that in Updegraph v. The Commonwealth, 11 S & R. 394, 400, it was decided that, "Christianity, general Christianity, is, and always has been, a part of the common law of Pennsylvania; . . . not Christianity with an established church, and tithes, and spiritual courts; but Christianity with liberty of conscience to all men." . . .
>
> If we pass beyond these matters to a view of American life as expressed by its laws, its business, its customs and its society, we find everywhere a clear recognition of the same truth. . . . These, and many other matters which might be noticed, add a volume of unofficial declarations to the mass of organic utterances that *this is a Christian nation.* In the face of all these, shall it be believed that a Congress of the United States intended to make it a misdemeanor for a church of this country to contract for the services of a Christian minister residing in another nation?[12] (Italics added).

The idea that Christian principles underlie American society was reiterated as to the State of Virginia, whence had come Madison and Jefferson, by the Virginia Supreme Court of Appeals in 1922:

> But *from the creation of the state until the present time, this state has been recognized as a Christian state,* at least in the sense that the great body of its citizens adhere to the tenets of the Christian religion; and, while at all times according freedom of conscience to all men, it has so far respected the opinions of this great body of its citizens as always to preserve from desecration the sanctity of Sunday, which they regard as holy[13] (Italics added).

More widely known is the dictum of Mr. Justice Douglas, speaking for the Court in *Zorach v. Clauson*[14] in 1952, that "We are a religious people whose institutions presuppose a Supreme Being." Justice Clark, speaking for the Court, specifically adopted this statement in the 1963 Schempp case.[15] Mr. Justice Douglas repeated the *dictum* in his concurring opinion in the 1962 Regents' Prayer case, but in that opinion, as well as in the Schempp case, he expressed his belief that such "aids" to religion as tax exemptions, chaplains in the armed forces, and even the inscription, "In God We Trust," on currency are unconstitutional. He reached this conclusion by applying his belief that, "if a religious leaven is to be worked into the affairs of our people, it is to be done by individuals and groups, not by the Government."[16] Justice Douglas operates upon the principle that all government financing of religion is unconstitutional. It is in the extraordinarily broad application he makes of that principle that his position betrays its vulnerability. Clearly, he has given insufficient weight to the meaning of American historical traditions and the distinction between governmental promotion of recognition of God, on the one hand, and governmental favoritism toward a particular sect on the other. And yet, even in his Regents' Prayer opinion, Mr. Justice Douglas reaffirmed that "We are a religious people whose institutions presuppose a Supreme Being," and Mr. Justice Black, for the majority of the Court in the Regents' Prayer case, observed, "The history of man is inseparable from the history of religion."[17] Or, as Mr. Justice Clark noted for the Court in the Schempp case, "today, as in the beginning, our national life reflects a religious people who, in the words of Madison, are "earnestly praying, as . . . in duty bound, that the Supreme Lawgiver of the Universe . . . guide them into every measure which may be worthy of his . . . blessing. . . ."[18] A point for discussion, therefore, is not whether we are a religious people who believe in God, but rather how it came about that we are forbidden to affirm that fact in our public life. The Supreme Court in the Schempp case justified this paradox by invoking the ideal of religious freedom: "This is not to say, however, that religion has been so identified with our history and government that religious freedom is not likewise as strongly imbedded in our public and private life."[19] Unfortunately, the Court finds no room for a "religious freedom" of the majority to express in public life the acknowledged religious elements of our heritage. And why, it should be asked, was the veto power of the uncoerced minority not discovered by the Supreme Court until the First Amendment was one hundred-seventy-one years old?

RECOGNITION BY AMERICAN LEADERS

In the preceding two sections we have recounted some of the "organic utterances" in constitutions, legislation and judicial decisions, testifying to the religious basis of American society. It remains to canvass a few expressed opinions of men who have been leaders of the American community. In them, further evidence will be found that the recurrent public acknowledgments of God and His position are more than ritualistic and are, rather, expressive of a national consensus and indicative of a heretofore conceded power in government to promote a proper observance of our relation to the Creator.

President George Washington included in his Farewell Address a testimonial to the necessity of a religious foundation for "political prosperity" in the following passage:

> Of all the dispositions and habits, which lead to political prosperity, religion and morality are indispensable supports. In vain would that man claim the tribute of patriotism, who should labor to subvert these great pillars of human happiness, these firmest props of the duties of men and citizens. The mere politician, equally with the pious man, ought to respect and cherish them. A volume could not trace all their connexions with private and public felicity. Let it simply be asked, Where is the security for property, for reputation, for life, if the sense of religious obligation desert the oaths, which are the instruments of investigation in courts of justice? And let us with caution indulge the supposition, that morality can be maintained without religion. Whatever may be conceded to the influence of refined education on minds of peculiar structure, reason and experience both forbid us to expect, that national morality can prevail in exclusion of religious principle.

This thought was echoed by Daniel Webster:

> . . . if we and our posterity be true to the Christian religion; if we and they shall live always in the fear of God, and shall respect his commandments; if we and they shall maintain just moral sentiments, and such conscientious convictions of duty as shall control the heart and life, we may have the highest hopes of the future fortunes of our country; and if we maintain those institutions of government and that political union exceeding all praise as much as it exceeds all former examples of political associations, we may be sure of one thing—that while our country furnishes materials for a thousand masters of the historic art, it will be no topic for a Gibbon, it will have no decline and fall. It will go on prospering and to prosper. But if we and our posterity reject religious instruction and authority, violate the rules of external justice, trifle with the injunctions of morality, and recklessly destroy the political constitution which holds us together, no man can tell how sudden a catastrophe may overwhelm us that shall bury all our glory in profound obscurity.[20]

Abraham Lincoln expressed his opinion, in his first inaugural address, that "Intelligence, patriotism, Christianity, and a firm reliance on Him who has never yet forsaken this favored land, are still competent to adjust, in the best way, all our present difficulty." Similarly, in his immortal Gettysburg Address, Lincoln offered hope "that this Nation under God, shall have a new birth of freedom, and that government of the people, by the people and for the people shall not perish from the earth."

It was during the Administration of President Lincoln that Congress directed that the motto, "In God we Trust," be inscribed on our coins, a practice which has been followed ever since. It has now been challenged by Mr. Justice Douglas.

Every President, excepting only Thomas Jefferson and Andrew Jackson, has issued Thanksgiving proclamations. Every President, without exception, has invoked God in his inaugural address. Extracts from those addresses are collected in *Appendix C*.

Woodrow Wilson, twenty-eighth President of the United

States, noted that: "America was born a Christian nation. America was born to exemplify that devotion to the elements of righteousness which are derived from the Holy Scriptures."[21]

In a more immediate setting, Astronaut Colonel John H. Glenn Jr. said, "Freedom, devotion to God and country are not things of the past. They will never become old-fashioned." The assassination of President John F. Kennedy was followed by a period of mourning in which officials at all levels of government joined with private citizens in offering prayers for him and the nation. The late President's last undelivered address concluded with the Biblical warning, "Except the Lord keep the city, the watchman waketh but in vain." Significantly, the newly-sworn President, Lyndon B. Johnson, concluded his first public statement as President—written aboard the plane speeding him from Dallas to Washington—with a frank, theistic avowal: "I will do my best. That is all I can do. I ask for your help—and God's." And President Johnson closed his first, formal address to Congress, on November 27, 1963, by quoting from the hymn, "America":

America, America
God shed His grace on thee,
And crown thy good
With brotherhood
From sea to shining sea.

JEFFERSON AND MADISON

Those who would debar the government from publicly recognizing God and His authority, frequently summon certain opinions of Thomas Jefferson and James Madison as proof that such recognition is proscribed by the letter of the First Amendment and is alien to the American tradition of liberty. In this discussion of the views of some leading Americans, it is imperative to note the expressed ideas of Jefferson and Madison, to aid in the refinement of the principles involved and especially to test the conclusions we have drawn.

During their presidencies, Jefferson and Madison were averse to proclaiming days of fast, prayer and thanksgiving. President Jefferson wrote a letter in 1802 to the Baptist Association of Danbury, Connecticut, in which he advanced, for the first time, his famed "wall of separation" metaphor to explain his constitutional scruples about proclaiming a national day of fast and prayer. The letter said in relevant part:

> Believing with you that religion is a matter which lies solely between man and his God, that he owes account to none other for his faith or his worship, that the legislative powers of government reach actions only, and not opinions, I contemplate with sovereign reverence that act of the whole American people which declared that their legislature should "make no law respecting an establishment of religion, or prohibiting the free exercise thereof," thus building a wall of separation between church and state. Adhering to this expression of the supreme will of the nation *on behalf of the rights of conscience,* I shall see with sincere satisfaction the progress of those sentiments which tend to restore to man all his natural rights . . ."[22] (Italics added).

Jefferson reiterated his position on Presidential thanksgiving proclamations in a letter to Reverend Samuel Miller in 1808:

> Certainly, no power to prescribe any religious exercise, or to assume authority in religious discipline, has been delegated to the General Government. . . . I do not believe it is for the interest of religion to invite the civil magistrate to direct its exercises, its discipline, or its doctrines; nor of the religious societies, that the General Government should be invested with the power of effecting any uniformity of time or matter among them. Fasting and praying are religious exercises; the enjoining them an act of discipline. Every religious society has a right to determine for itself the times for these exercises, and the objects proper for them, according to their own particular tenets. . . ."[23]

When Jefferson was Governor of Virginia, however, he readily issued proclamations, such as that of November 11, 1779, decreeing a day "of publick and solemn thanksgiving and prayer to Almighty God."[24] President Jefferson included a prayer in each of his two inaugural addresses. He signed bills appropriating money for chaplains in Congress and the armed services, and signed the Articles of War, which not only provided for chaplains but also "earnestly recommended to all officers and soldiers, diligently to attend divine services."[25] In 1803, he signed an appropriation of funds to be paid to the Catholic Church for the education and religious training of the Kaskaskia Indians, pursuant to an 1803 treaty with that tribe which provided:

> And whereas the greater part of the said tribe have been baptized and received into the Catholic Church, to which they are much attached, the United States will give annually, for seven years, one hundred dollars toward the support of a priest of that religion, who will engage to perform for said tribe the duties of his office, and also to instruct as many of their children as possible, in the rudiments of literature, and the United States will further give the sum of three hundred dollars, to assist the said tribe in the erection of a church.[26]

Through the 1830's, incidentally, all the principal religious denominations, including the Congregationalists, Baptists, Methodists, Presbyterians, Moravians, Episcopalians and Catholics, accepted various federal funds for the education of Indians.[27]

During the exigency of the War of 1812, President Madison responded reluctantly to pressure from Congress to proclaim a day of public prayer. Madison's proclamation recommended a specific day for prayer, but he made it clear that his recommendation was directed only to those who voluntarily would wish to join, and that the sponsorship and composition of the prayers would be by the people and their congregations, not by the government. After leaving office, Madison noted, in his Detached Memoranda written in 1820, that he felt prayer and thanksgiving proclamations to be beyond the proper role of government because of, among other reasons, the "tendency of the practice, to narrow the recommendation to the standard of the predominant sect," and because the "practice if not strictly guarded naturally terminates in a conformity to the creed of the majority and a single sect, if amounting to a majority." He explained his reluctant proclamation, as President, of a day of prayer in this way:

> It was thought not proper to refuse a compliance altogether; but a form & language were employed, which were meant to deaden as much as possible any claim of political right to enjoin religious observances by resting these expressly on the

> voluntary compliance of individuals, and even by limiting the recommendation to such as wished simultaneous as well as voluntary performance of a religious act on the occasion.[28]

President Madison vetoed, on First Amendment grounds, a bill to incorporate an Episcopal Church in the District of Columbia, and he later expressed his view that the employment of chaplains in Congress and the armed forces is unconstitutional. He also believed that a gift of federal land to a Baptist Church in Mississippi violated the First Amendment, and vetoed a bill making the gift.[29]

These actions contrast with Madison's apparent attitude at the time the Constitution and First Amendment were drafted. For example, on May 9, 1787, Congress was petitioned to sell certain lands in each township of the Northwest Territory.[30] The matter was referred to a committee of which Madison was a member. On July 10, 1787, the committee, with Madison's concurrence, recommended the sale, with this condition: "The lot N29 in each township or fractional part of a township to be given perpetually for the purposes of religion."[31] Congress authorized the sale, with that provision, on July 23, 1787.[32] There is no record of any dissent by Madison. Madison's action here sharply differs from his later and perhaps over-scrupulous disclaimers.

Contrary to his later misgivings, Madison served in the First Congress on the committee to appoint a chaplain to Congress.[33] It is not recorded that he registered any objection. As President, he signed bills providing for chaplains in Congress and the armed forces. He also invoked the aid of God in his inaugural addresses.

Both Jefferson and Madison recognized the propriety of voluntary, sectarian religious exercises within the bounds of the University of Virginia, a state institution which Jefferson founded. Jefferson prepared a report for the Commissioners of the University, which was signed by Madison as a member of that body, and which said:

> It is supposed probable, that a building of somewhat more size in the middle of the grounds may be called for in time, in which may be rooms for *religious worship*, under such impartial regulations as the Visitors shall prescribe, for public

> examinations, for a library, for the schools of music, drawing, and other associated purposes[34] (Italics added).

As Rector of the University, Jefferson prepared the Regulations enacted by the Board of Visitors of the University on April 7, 1824, which were approved by Madison as a member of the Board. The regulations stated:

> Should the religious sects of this State, or any of them, according to the invitation held out to them, establish *within,* or adjacent to, the precincts of the University, schools for instruction in the religion of their sect, *the students of the University will be free, and expected to attend* religious worship at the establishment of their respective sects, in the morning, and in time to meet their school in the University at its stated hour.
>
> The students of such religious school, if they attend any school of the University, shall be considered as students of the University, subject to the same regulations, and entitled to the same rights and privileges.
>
> The upper circular room of the rotunda shall be reserved for a library.
>
> One of its larger elliptical rooms on its middle floor shall be used for annual examinations, for lectures to such schools as are too numerous for their ordinary school room, *and for religious worship,* under the regulations allowed to be prescribed by law[35] (Italics added).

While the states were not then subject to the strictures of the First Amendment, since the Fourteenth Amendment had not been enacted, and while the University of Virginia episode therefore did not involve a legal application of the First Amendment, yet the matter is instructive as an indication of the favorable attitudes of the two men toward some governmental encouragement and promotion of religion. It has been remarked, perhaps not wholly in jest, that Thomas Jefferson was one of the first advocates of a released time program.[36]

It is important to keep the views of Jefferson and Madison in perspective. Frequently, they are cited as definitive guides to the meaning of the First Amendment. The Bill of Rights, however, was the work of the First Congress and the ratifying state legislatures, and was not the product merely of Jefferson and Madison, notwithstanding their lofty eminence in the annals of their time. Jefferson, in fact, was absent in Europe during the Constitutional Convention of 1787, the ratification of the Constitution by the states, and the formulation of the First Amendment by the First Congress. It is evident that Jefferson, like Madison, envisioned the First Amendment primarily as a device to ensure freedom of conscience by maintaining an equality among religious sects. Although his "wall of separation" metaphor was described in a Supreme Court *dictum* in 1879 "almost as an authoritative declaration of the scope and effect of the amendment,"[37] it is unlikely that Jefferson would have pushed his metaphor to the point where an overzealous separation of church and state actually interfered with the "rights of conscience," which he described in the same passage as the main beneficiaries of the First Amendment. It would distort his position to present Jefferson as building a wall of separation so tight that the government would be inhibited from acknowledging God even where the acknowledgment could be made without significantly imperiling those "rights of conscience." Similarly, the later misgivings of Madison ought not to dictate our interpretation of the First Amendment as drafted by the Congress and ratified by the state legislatures. Madison appears to have acceded at the time to the several actions of the First Congress in recognition of God and in the promotion of general religion, just as Jefferson's attitude toward public days of fast and thanksgiving was favorable during the Revolutionary War.

It is fair to conclude that the later and limited trepidations of Jefferson and Madison ought not to outbalance the obvious general intent of the framers of the Constitution and First Amendment. The First Congress, as we have seen, called on the President to proclaim a day of public prayer and did so on the very day it approved the First Amendment. The setting and conduct of the state conventions indicate that they, too, considered government recognition of God to be fully consonant with the letter and spirit of the Constitution. The New York Convention, for example, which ratified the Constitution on July 26, 1788, proposed an amendment to the

Constitution to safeguard the free exercise of religion and to ensure "that no Religious Sect or Society ought to be favored or established by Law in preference of others." Yet that Convention ordered, on its opening day, that "the Business of this Convention be opened every morning with Prayer" by a clergyman.[38]

When we balance the probabilities, we find that the indicated intent of the First Amendment, the historical setting of its birth, and the impressive assent of subsequent American leaders, clearly outweigh the reservations of Jefferson and Madison.

III

1. Report 376. 32nd Cong., 2nd Session, 4.
2. See "Religious Education," May–June, 1961.
3. See Proposed Amendments to the Constitution, H. R. Doc. No. 551, (70th Cong., 2nd Sess.), 182.
4. 4 Cong. Rec. 5453.
5. *Ibid.*
6. See 4 Cong. Rec. 5588.
7. *People v. Ruggles,* 8 Johns. (N.Y.) 290, 293 (1811).
8. *Vidal et al. v. Girard's Executors,* 43 U.S. 126, 198 (1844).
9. *Ibid.*
10. 143 U.S. 457 (1892).
11. 143 U.S. at 465.
12. 143 U.S. at 470–471.
13. *Pirkey Bros. v. Commonwealth,* 134 Va. 713, 717, 114 S.E. 764, 765 (1922).
14. 343 U.S. 306, 313 (1952).
15. 374 U.S. at 213.
16. *Engel v. Vitale,* 370 U.S. 421, 443 (1962).
17. *Engel v. Vitale,* 370 U.S. 421, 434 (1962).
18. 374 U.S. at 213.
19. 374 U.S. at 214.
20. Johnson, Chaplains of the General Government (1856), 55.
21. Martin, *Our Public Schools—Christian or Secular* (1952), 65.
22. Healey, *Jefferson on Religion in Public Education* (New Haven, 1962), 131–132.
23. Writings (Bergh, ed., 1903), XI, 428–429.
24. *The Papers of Thomas Jefferson* (Boyd, ed. 1951), III, 178.
25. Act of April 10, 1806, C. 20, 2 Stat. 359, 360.
26. See Costanzo, Federal Aid to Education and Religious Liberty, 36 *U. of Det. L. J.*, 1, 15 (1958).
27. See Beaver, "Church, State and the Indians: Indian Missions in the New Nation," 4 *Journal of Church and State,* 11, 23–24 (1962).

28. For the text of the church-state portion of Madison's Detached Memoranda, see Cahn, "On Government and Prayer," 37 *N.Y. Univ. L. Rev.* 981, 995 (1962).
29. See Writings of James Madison, Hunt ed. (New York, 1900–1910), VIII, 133.
30. Journals of the Continental Congress, XXXII, 276.
31. *Ibid.,* XXXII, 312.
32. *Ibid.,* XXXIII, 399.
33. Annals of Congress, I, 109.
34. Honeywell, *The Educational Work of Thomas Jefferson* (1931), 249.
35. *Ibid.,* 274–275.
36. Meiklejohn, "Educational Cooperation Between Church and State," 14 *Law & Contemp. Prob.* 61, 69 (1949).
37. *Reynolds v. the United States,* 98 U.S. 145, 164 (1879).
38. Journals of the Proceedings of the Convention of the State of New York (1788), June 17, 1788.

And whereas it is the duty of nations as well as of men to own their dependence upon the over-ruling power of God, . . . and to recognize the sublime truth, announced in the Holy Scriptures and proven by all history, that those nations only are blessed whose God is the Lord. . . .

ABRAHAM LINCOLN
Proclamation of April 30, 1863

IV

Can Government Be Neutral?

The First Amendment works to prohibit "an establishment of religion." In 1878, the Supreme Court ruled that the meaning of "religion" in the First Amendment can best be found in "the history of the times in the midst of which the provision was adopted."[1] As we have seen, "establishment of religion" connoted, at the time of the adoption of the Amendment, the attribution of a preferred status to one or more favored sects among the many groups professing a belief in God. Similarly, the "free exercise of religion" protected in the second clause of the Amendment referred to the exercise of an individual's belief in or about God. As the Supreme Court put it in 1890: "The term "religion" has reference to one's views of his relations to his Creator, and to the obligations they impose of reverence for his being and character, and of obedience to his will."[2]

Under this definition, which is narrow but practically self-evident in its ordinary meaning, atheism and agnosticism would not be considered religions and therefore a bare governmental recognition of God could not be assailed under either religious clause of the First Amendment as a disparagement of atheism and agnosticism. This definition, which assumes that a belief in God is the common denominator of all "religions," has now been altered by the Supreme Court, so that professions which do not acknowledge the existence of

God may now be considered religions and may claim the full protection accorded to religions by the First Amendment.

In the 1961 case of *Torcaso v. Watkins,*[3] the Supreme Court invalidated a provision of the Constitution of Maryland requiring a state employee to declare his belief in God. The test, said Mr. Justice Black for the Court, unconstitutionally invaded the employee's " freedom of belief and religion."[4] The requirement is invalid because "The power and authority of the State of Maryland thus is put on the side of one particular sort of believers—those who are willing to say they believe in 'the existence of God.' "[5] The Court went on to spell out the entitlement of non-theistic beliefs to protection as religions:

> We repeat and again reaffirm that neither a State nor the Federal Government can constitutionally force a person "to profess his belief or disbelief in any religion." Neither can constitutionally pass laws or impose requirements which aid all religions as against non-believers, and *neither can aid those religions based on a belief in the existence of God as against those religions founded on different beliefs*[6] (Italics added).

Appended to the last quoted clause was a footnote specifying that:

> Among religions in this country which do not teach what would commonly be considered a belief in the existence of God are Buddhism, Taoism, Ethical Culture, Secular Humanism and others.[7]

In view of this holding, it may now be said that there are two general types of religions entitled to the protections of the First Amendment. On the one hand are those which profess a belief in God. For purposes of discussion, let us call them theistic, and for analysis we shall include therein both deistic and theistic beliefs in God with their variant interpretations of the nature of God and his providence.[8] On the other hand are those non-theistic religions described in Mr. Justice Black's footnote in the Torcaso case. Of the four he mentioned, the two most important in contemporary terms are Ethical Culture and Secular Humanism. Ethical Culture has been described as follows:

> The Society for Ethical Culture was founded in the Spring of 1876 by Dr. Felix Adler. Its adherents maintain that the true test of religious consecration must be what men do for one another in their day-by-day living to achieve mutually creative and liberating relationships. Drawing inspiration and guidance from the great men in every age, this religious and educational fellowship, respecting the dignity and worth of every individual, seeks to develop ethical values in human relations. Without formal creed, it dedicates itself "to the ever increasing knowledge and practice and love of the right."[9]

Secular Humanism operates on a similar rationale:

> Humanism is a faith in people, in all humanity, and in science as a means of attaining truth. It is also a quest for the ethical and spiritual values of life through philosophy, science, the arts and literature. Humanists in general are not interested in supposedly supernatural phenomena nor in conventional religion and they are opposed to any form of authoritarian control. Most of them are individually active in expressing these ideas in some form of social action or education that promotes human dignity and enriches the content of life on earth.[10]

Ethical Culture and Secular Humanism, then, may be called non-theistic religions in that they do not affirm the existence of God. It is reasonable also to include unorganized atheism and agnosticism within the broad Torcaso description of non-theistic religions. While atheism positively rejects a belief in God's existence, agnosticism is: "The doctrine that neither the existence nor the nature of God, nor the ultimate origin of the universe, is known or knowable. . . ."[11] Atheism and agnosticism are fully compatible with Ethical Culture and Secular Humanism. Moreover, less organized atheists and agnostics ought to be as much entitled to First Amendment protection as Ethical Culturists or Secular Humanists. If the latter beliefs are to be regarded as religions, so too should the atheistic and agnostic creeds even when they appear in their elemental philosophical state wholly devoid of organizational trappings. The First Amendment, therefore, should protect equally the free exercise of atheism, Ethical Culture and Presbyterianism. And it should also prevent a preferential establishment of any of them.

The Supreme Court in the 1963 Schempp case quoted approvingly the Torcaso dictum that government cannot "aid those religions based on a belief in the existence of God as against those religions founded on different beliefs,"[12] thereby reaffirming the constitutional status of non-theistic religions. The formal treatment of non-theistic creeds as religions proceeds from a recognition that those beliefs have now attained a status and influence that they lacked in the early days of the Republic. Although the Supreme Court in the Schempp case reaffirmed that, "We are a religious people whose institutions presuppose a Supreme Being,"[13] Mr. Justice Brennan's concurring opinion cut more cleanly to the deeper meaning of the Torcaso and school prayer decisions. For one thing, the Court has, properly, acknowledged the greater religious diversity in America today. As Mr. Justice Brennan put it:

> (O)ur religious composition makes us a vastly more diverse people than were our forefathers. They knew differences chiefly among Protestant sects. Today the Nation is far more heterogeneous religiously, including as it does substantial minorities not only of Catholics and Jews but as well of those who worship according to no version of the Bible and those who worship no God at all. See Torcaso v. Watkins, 367 US 488, 495.[14]

In view of this increased variety in our religious composition, it is quite proper for the court to extend the protection of the free exercise clause to non-theistic religions, and to construe the establishment clause to bar a law respecting a real "establishment," in the limited historical sense of the word, of either a theistic or a non-theistic religion. The Court, however, has gone much further, and has translated the increase of non-theistic religions into a warrant to declare that the formerly acknowledged American heritage itself is irrelevant or dead insofar as it countenances any meaningful public recognition of God and His place. Thus it is that Mr. Justice Brennan in the Schempp case asserts the duty of public schools to provide "an atmosphere in which children may assimilate a heritage common to all American groups and religions. . . . This is a heritage neither theistic nor atheistic, but simply civic and patriotic."[15] What is more, the Court seems bent upon construing the First Amendment to conform to its own current estimate of the changing religious complexion of American life rather than to the original substantial meaning of the Amendment itself. At least the Brennan opinion so indicates:

> In the face of such profound changes, practices which may have been objectionable to no one in the time of Jefferson and Madison may today be highly offensive to many persons, the deeply devout and the nonbelievers alike.[16]

In summary, the new standard erected by the Court broadens the prior meaning of "religion" so that the various non-theistic beliefs and believers stand on an equal First Amendment footing with the traditional theistic religions and their adherents. The new rule would seem to require, then, that the imperatives of the establishment clause of the First Amendment, which traditionally sought to ensure neutrality among sects of theistic religions, must now be applied to achieve neutrality between these two classes of "sects," the theistic "sect" on the one hand and the non-theistic on the other. This is the neutrality the Court pursued in the school prayer cases. If such neutrality is impossible of practical achievement, then is the new definition of religion untenable? Or does the guarantee of neutrality implicit in the First Amendment not apply as between the two broad classes of theistic and non-theistic religions?

It is commonly said that government in the United States must be impartial in religious matters. Historically, this has meant there ought to be no official favoritism toward any one or several of the various denominations professing a belief in God. In the past, the notion of neutrality has allowed in practice that the government could seek to articulate, in its public utterances, a common denominator among Christian religions. Heretofore, this has ordinarily meant a belief in God and a generalized reverence for the Old and New Testaments. Today, the rhetoric of neutrality is still employed in spite of the recognition of non-theistic professions as religions.

The Supreme Court has now placed all religions on a parity, whether Christian, non-Christian theistic, or non-theistic.

On the merits of the question, it is fair to define religion, for some First Amendment purposes, broadly enough to include a loyalty to ultimate values even if the source of those values is not divine in the traditional sense. Common sense impels the conclusion that an atheist is entitled to the "free exercise" of his atheism, in that he may not be compelled to profess or practice a theistic creed, and he may put his atheistic beliefs into practice subject to the same requirements of the common good which inhibit the outward practices of all religions. But a real problem arises under the establishment clause of the First Amendment from the Court's adoption, without limitation, of the supposed parity of theistic and non-theistic religions. If, as the Supreme Court now indicates, theistic and non-theistic religions are merely different sects among religions, then would not a governmental recognition of God be a patronage of theistic sects and a disparagement of the non-theistic? Obviously, it logically would and government would thereby forfeit its neutrality among religions, a neutrality which, according to the Court, must be strictly maintained.

In the nature of things, however, governmental favor of one side or the other, the theistic or the non-theistic, cannot be avoided in logic or practice. To illustrate, suppose that a school child asks his public school teacher, "Is the Declaration of Independence true when it says that men are endowed by their Creator with certain unalienable rights?" Or, more starkly, "Is there a God?" The questions would seem to be licit inquiries in an educational process designed to explore the truth, and therefore they cannot be dismissed out of hand as impertinent or irrelevant. Now let us consider the possible answers. If the teacher says, "Yes, the Declaration is true in that respect," or says, "Yes, there is a God," he is obviously aligning himself, and the government he represents, on the side of theism. If he answers "no" to both questions, he is just as clearly lining the government up on the side of atheism with its denial of the existence of God. In either case the government, through its teacher, is preferring theistic or non-theistic religion. A third approach would be for the teacher to say, "I don't know," or, "I cannot say whether it is true or not, because the government cannot take a postion on the existence of God." In this way, it seems plain, the teacher is aligning the government on the side of agnosticism through his affirmation that, as a matter of state policy, God's existence is unknown or unknowable. And since agnosticism, as we have seen, may be properly classified as a non-theistic religion, the government here again favors non-theistic religion.

It is contended by some that the government does maintain true neutrality between theistic and non-theistic religions when it adopts this third, agnostic approach. It is said that all religions, whether they recognize God or not, do avow in common certain ethical and moral principles, such as fairness, respect for the rights of others, obedience to law, etc. By espousing these common tenets, while abstaining from introducing the divisive element of God, the government, according to this notion, can enrich the moral tone of the community without engendering disruptive religious controversy. The argument, it must be conceded, has a deceptively plausible ring. Especially is this so in an age where the avoidance of controversy has become something of an end in itself.

There is, however, a fatal defect in this approach. Theistic and non-theistic religions do agree, it is true, on certain ethical and moral principles. It may even be said, without unduly stretching the point, that generally they agree that men are possessed of "certain unalienable rights," as the Declaration of Independence affirmed. But it would be unrealistic to think that the principles of morality, justice and human rights can be taught without ever adverting to their source. Indeed, it is fair to say that the question of source must be answered before the affirmation of principles and rights can be made with any force or particularity as to the extent of their application. For example, if the source of "unalienable" rights is a divine lawgiver who has ordained the character of those rights, their durability would seem to be greater than in the case where the source of rights is found in an individual contractual assent, which can be revoked, or in a simple majority rule. Moreover, it would not be irrelevant for a school child to ask his teacher whence come those commonly acknowledged principles and rights which the teacher extols. Specifically, he could rightly ask: "Do they come from God?"

The question would have to be answered. As with the basic question of the existence of God, neutrality between theistic and non-theistic religions would appear to be unattainable. If the teacher affirms that the Declaration of Independence is true, and that men are given the rights "by their Creator," he is advancing theism as truth. If he answers flatly, "No, there is no God," he espouses atheism. If he says that the rights originate in some non-divine source, such as a consensus, or human nature, or the Constitution, he is negatively stating a judgment as to the nature of God and, by his implicit denial that there is a God who has the attribute of a giver of rights, he parallels to that extent the atheistic or agnostic position and diverges from the theistic as stated in the Declaration of Independence. And if he says, "Go ask your mother. The government cannot take a position on whether rights come from God," then he aligns the government squarely on the side of agnosticism.

Those who would remove all prayer from the schools and other public functions would have government, through the silence of its public officials, espouse atheism or agnosticism. This is so because the silent but studied refusal to recognize God raises an inference either that He does not exist or that His existence is debatable as a matter of state policy and therefore not a fit subject for an official public affirmation. To be sure, the Supreme Court would not permit an open avowal by government of atheism as truth. As the Schempp Court said: "We agree of course that the State may not establish a "religion of secularism" in the sense of affirmatively opposing or showing hostility to religion, thus "preferring those who believe in no religion over those who do believe."[17] The Court, however, apparently requires public officials to maintain silence or a non-committal posture on the question of God's existence. And while the Court may wish this to be an essentially agnostic position, in which no judgment is made as to whether God exists, yet there is a likelihood that some, especially school children, will construe it as an atheistic denial by the state of God's existence.

In either case, the adoption of the atheistic or agnostic view on the existence of God is an irretrievable repudiation of theistic religion and a preference of the non-theistic. The coincidence between theistic and non-theistic religions on collateral points, such as their mutual recognition of some human rights, cannot obscure the fact that, on the basic point of division between the two, one or the other must be preferred. If, on the major point of its conflict with theistic religion—that is, the question of the existence of God—the government, by its affirmation or abstention, adopts the view of non-theistic religion, and thereafter espouses only subordinate principles common to both, affirming nothing inconsistent with the non-theistic view, it seems clear that government has preferred non-theistic religion. This is so despite the incidental congruences of the two types of religion on collateral points.

And so it is, that the Supreme Court, while invoking the rhetoric of an impossible "neutrality," has neatly replaced our traditional public affirmation of God and His law with a new, non-theistic public creed, demanding of the state a perpetual suspension of judgment on the question: "Is there a God?"

IV

1. *Reynolds v. U.S.* 98 U.S. 145, 162 (1878).
2. *Davis v. Beason* 133 U.S. 333, 342 (1890).
3. 367 U.S. 488 (1961).
4. 367 U.S. at 496.
5. 367 U.S. at 490.
6. 367 U.S. at 495.
7. 367 U.S. at 495.
8. See the discussion of deistic and theistic references in the Declaration of Independence above on page 29.
9. Randall, *The Ethical Challenge of a Pluralistic Society* (New York, 1959), p. 2.
10. *The Humanist,* March–April, May–June, 1962.
11. *Webster's New International Dictionary, Unabridged* (Second Edition).
12. 374 U.S. at 220.
13. 374 U.S. at 213.
14. 374 U.S. at 239–240.
15. 374 U.S. at 242.
16. 374 U.S. at 240.
17. 374 U.S. at 225.

On the other hand, other language of the amendment commands that [a state] cannot hamper its citizens in the free exercise of their own religion. Consequently, it cannot exclude individual Catholics, Lutherans, Mohammedans, Baptists, Jews, Methodists, Non-believers, Presbyterians, or the members of any other faith, because of their faith or lack of it, *from receiving the benefits of public welfare legislation.*

MR. JUSTICE BLACK
in Everson v. Board of Education (1947)

V

Effect of Decisions on Federal Aid to Church-related Schools

PRELIMINARY CONSIDERATIONS

Analytically and practically, the school prayer cases signal a preference by the federal government of the non-theistic, secular approach to the ultimate questions of life. In its effort to inhibit the state from passing judgment on even the most basic religious question—the existence of God—the Supreme Court in reality has enjoined upon government a predictably non-theistic, agnostic mandate in all public religious matters. Under the guise of impartial suspension of judgment, the Court has ordained as a constitutional imperative that the agnostic approach is true, and therefore that the theistic is wrong. It would be going too far, as we have seen, to say that the Court has institutionalized atheism. Indeed the rationale of the decisions would clearly interdict an explicit affirmation by government that God in fact does not exist. But that the school prayer decisions do betoken an agnostic, non-theistic approach that is logically at war with the theistic, is rather clear.

It follows that the official rejection of theism, and adoption of non-theism, as the constitutional touchstone in religious matters, warrants the exclusion from public life of official practices conflicting with that non-theistic approach. For we are dealing with the First Amendment, where the limitations, once defined, will be jealously enforced without delay. Moreover, since tradition and apparent contemporary public opinion support the Court-rejected theistic grounding of society, the only way to implement the non-theistic mandate will be, not through the unlikely voluntary adoption of it by the people, but through active promotion by government. It must be recalled, too, that government, especially the federal government, has at its command not only the twentieth-century engines of propaganda and news management with which to engender public acquiescence, but also the ultimate coercive power inherent in all governments.

Change by evolution can be gradual, tested by experience in the process, and tempered by the practicalities of life in an ordered world. But the Court here appears to demand a change in settled patterns not by evolution, but by revolution. The sword of this revolution is the abstraction. The Supreme Court by abstract and over-literal interpretations in religious and other matters, has been engaged "in a species of absolutism in it reasonings which is more likely to lead us into darkness than to light."[1] Abstractions, once set in motion and freed from the prudential restraints of common sense and experience, can lead to mischief. So it is that the trend begun by the school prayer decisions can result, unless checked, in consequences which are as repugnant to the reasonable man as they are inevitable to the abstractionist. To these consequences, we shall turn our attention in this and the succeeding two chapters.

THE AID CONTROVERSY AND THE COURT

An early casualty of the absolutist attack may be any attempt to include sectarian schools in general federal aid to education. There have been efforts to identify the movement supporting public prayer with the movement seeking public funds for sectarian schools. Mr. Justice Rutledge linked the two in his dissenting opinion in the Everson case in 1947:

> Two great drives are constantly in motion to abridge, in the name of education, the complete division of religion and civil authority which our forefathers made. One is to introduce religious education and observances into the public schools. The other, to obtain public funds for the aid and support of various private religious schools. . . . In my opinion both

> avenues were closed by the Constitution. Neither should be opened by this Court.[2]

More recent evaluations have outrun the Rutledge notation of the alleged coincidence between the drives for public prayer and public funds. Now, it is frankly, and incorrectly, asserted by some that proponents of public prayer are in fact motivated, not by the considerations they advance in argument, but rather by a covert desire for federal aid to sectarian schools. For example, in an article on July 12, 1962 in the *Baptist Press,* W. Barry Garrett, Washington regional editor, observed:

> The Roman Catholic hierarchy has been bitter in criticism of the Court's decision. This is to be expected. The cardinals see their campaign for Federal aid to parochial schools disappearing as vapor on a hot summer day. This decision makes the Catholic Church's chances for aid from the Federal Government for its parochial schools almost nil.
>
> Already it has affected the bills on higher education that are tied up in conference committee between the House and Senate. A scheduled meeting of the committee was postponed a week in order for the Court's decision to be studied. Even spokesmen in the House for Federal grants to church-related colleges are pessimistic about their chances. The Court's decision will affect elementary and secondary parochial schools even more directly.
>
> It is no wonder that the Roman Catholic clergy is attacking the decision.[3]

Similarly, Protestants and Other Americans United for Separation of Church and State commented on *Engel v. Vitale:*

> Believers in church-state separation will be heartened by this decision in their endeavor to hold the "money line" between state and church. *Those who had hoped to advance public money for parochial schools by legislating a government-composed prayer will be disappointed.* The attempt failed. Justice Black, speaking for the Court, gives every evidence not of relaxing but rather of tightening the ban on state aid to church institutions which he has repeatedly asserted in other opinions.

> This matter receives even sharper articulation in the concurring opinion of Justice Douglas which stresses the unconstitutionality of money involvement between state and church. It is the expenditure of public funds to support a religious exercise, he declares, which provides the decisive constitutional test. If the minuscule expenditure of public funds involved in the preparation and implementation of the regents' prayer renders this program unconstitutional, then surely the channeling of many millions of dollars of public funds into church schools would be unconstitutional, as well.[4]

The logic of the school prayer decisions is sufficiently sweeping to forbid the extension of general federal aid to sectarian schools. The Court in the Schempp case noted that "this Court has rejected unequivocally the contention that the establishment clause forbids only governmental preference of one religion over another."[5] Instead, the Court reaffirmed the *obiter dictum* of the 1947 Everson case that neither a state nor the federal government "can pass laws which aid one religion, *aid all religions,* or prefer one religion over another" (Italics added).[6] Within this blanket prohibition, though, the Court has permitted legislation incidentally aiding religion if the enactment serves a primary secular purpose, and the Schempp Court has given a guideline for future cases:

> The test may be stated as follows: what are the purpose and the primary effect of the enactment? If either is the advancement or inhibition of religion then the enactment exceeds the scope of legislative power as circumscribed by the Constitution. That is to say that to withstand the strictures of the Establishment Clause *there must be a secular legislative purpose and a primary effect that neither advances nor inhibits religion. Everson v. Board of Education, supra: McGowan v. Maryland, supra.* at 442[7] (Italics added).

In the 1947 Everson and 1961 McGowan cases, which it cited to illustrate this principle, the Court upheld a New Jersey provision of bus transportation to parochial school students, and a series of Sunday-closing laws, on the theory that they served the valid secular purposes, respectively, of getting children safely to school and ensuring one day of rest a week. The benefits flowing to religion were treated as incidental. Everson and McGowan involved rather minor benefits to religion. There is no assurance that this Supreme Court would similarly uphold the inclusion of church-related schools in a massive program of federal aid to education. Such inclusion could readily be found to have, in the words of the Schempp Court, "a primary effect that . . . advances . . . religion." The fact that such aid would, in major effect, "aid those religions based on a belief in the existence of God as against those religions founded on different beliefs," as the Court put it in the Torcaso and Schempp cases, could have an important bearing on the decision.

THE PRECEDENTS

There are several types of federal aid proposals, including grants or loans to the schools or the students themselves, and the treatment of a taxpayer's educational expenditures, or school taxes he has paid, as deductible from his taxable income or as a credit directly against his federal income tax. The tax deduction and tax credit proposals are subject to fewer constitutional objections than grants or loans. This discussion, moreover, will assume that the general federal aid program under discussion includes grants or loans to parochial schools. But it is not the purpose here to examine the fine points of the question. Rather, our inquiry is mainly whether the Constitution forbids *all* such federal grants or loans to parochial schools. It is fair to say that a decision invalidating the inclusion of parochial schools in such a general program of federal aid to education, at least where the aid is for a primary secular purpose, would entail a disregard by the Court of a number of related precedents. Most leading contemporary experts, including Professors Arthur E. Sutherland and Mark DeWolfe Howe of Harvard Law School, Wilber G. Katz of the University of Chicago, Paul G. Kauper of the University of Michigan, and others, recognize a limited power in Congress to accomplish a public purpose through support of at least the essentially nonsectarian activities of church-related schools. The relevant case law would seem to support their conclusions. In 1899, in *Bradfield v. Roberts,*[8] the Supreme Court upheld a Congressional appropriation to erect a hospital building for an order of Roman Catholic nuns. The Court thus approved a direct appropriation, for the performance of the public function of caring for the sick poor, to an institution conducted under the auspices of a church which exercised, in the Court's phrase, "perhaps controlling influence" over it.

In 1930, in *Cochran v. Board of Education,*[9] the Court held it constitutional for Louisiana to provide secular textbooks for parochial school children. The decision indicates that the teaching of secular subjects in parochial schools is the performance of a public function and that it may therefore be governmentally aided. This case was decided before the Court had flatly held that the restrictions of the First Amendment were made fully applicable to the states by the Fourteenth Amendment. If Cochran were an isolated holding, it would not be a strong precedent today, now that the Court holds that the states are fully bound by the stricter standards of the First Amendment. But in fact it is not an isolated holding, as indicated by the Everson case in 1947.

In *Everson v. Board of Education,*[10] the Court held that a New Jersey statute providing for reimbursement of bus transportation costs by the state to parents of children attending parochial schools was constitutional. The reimbursement undeniably made it easier for the parents to send their children to the church-related schools and therefore it conferred a definite though unmeasurable benefit upon the religious institutions. The actual holding, then, reinforces the rule of Bradfield and Cochran that a financial benefit may constitutionally be conferred upon a religious body incidentally to the achievement of a public purpose. Mr. Justice Black, however, speaking for the Court, delivered himself of unfortunately sweeping language that was not necessary to the decision of the case. He said in one place: "The 'establishment of religion' clause of the First Amendment means at least this: Neither a state nor the Federal Government can set up a church. Neither can pass laws which aid one religion, *aid all religions,* or prefer one religion over another" (Italics added).[11] This language was adopted by the Court in the Schempp case. Unhappily, another passage of the Black opinion in Everson is less frequently quoted:

> On the other hand, other language of the amendment commands that New Jersey cannot hamper its citizens in the free exercise of their own religion. Consequently, it cannot exclude individual Catholics, Lutherans, Mohammedans, Baptists, Jews, Methodists, Non-believers, Presbyterians, or the members of any other faith, *because of their faith or lack of it,* from receiving the benefits of public welfare legislation.[12] (Italics in original.)

This principle is compelling in its fairness and it could serve to validate the inclusion of parochial schools in a program of general federal aid to education, as well as their inclusion in ancillary programs such as the provision of transportation. It is significant that the Supreme Court reaffirmed this principle, and quoted that very language from the Everson case, in a decision it rendered on the same day as the Schempp decision. The case was *Sherbet v. Verner,*[13] in which a Seventh Day Adventist sought unemployment compensation under the South Carolina law. Pursuant to her faith, however, she refused to accept any job which would require her to work on Saturdays. The state officials found that this was a failure "without good cause, . . . to accept available suitable work,"[14] and therefore that she was ineligible for benefits. The Supreme Court, in an opinion by Mr. Justice Brennan, held that this was an invalid infringement upon the petitioner's free exercise of religion, in that the state denied her the benefits of public welfare legislation because she followed a dictate of her faith. It could readily follow that parochial school children could not be denied inclusion in a program of general aid to education because their faith impelled them to attend religious schools. Thus, it could be argued, not only that inclusion of parochial schools in federal aid would be constitutional, but also that their exclusion would be invalid.

Mr. Justice Stewart wrote a concurring opinion in the Sherbert case in which he agreed that it violated the petitioner's free exercise of religion to be subjected to that economic disadvantage because of her faith. But he also, and properly, noted that the ruling of the Court in Sherbert contradicts what he called the Court's "insensitive and sterile construction of the Establishment Clause."[15] As he pointed out, the majority of the Court is fond of quoting extravagant dicta to the effect that the establishment clause forbids "every form of public aid or support for religion."[16] Yet, in Sherbert, the court compelled South Carolina to make an exception, on religious grounds, from its general rule that one who refuses employment for any personal reason is ineligible for unemployment compensation. Thus, South Carolina may deny benefits to an applicant who refuses a job because she cannot get a baby sitter, but may not deny them to an applicant who refuses the job for purely religious reasons. This is clearly an "aid" to religion, and a discriminatory one, at that, because it favors religions which prohibit work on Saturday. Yet the result in the Sherbert case is obviously reasonable and fair. Moreover, as Mr. Justice Stewart observed, "the Free Exercise Clause affirmatively requires government to create an atmosphere of hospitality and accommodation to individual belief and disbelief."[17] Yet, in the school prayer cases, the free exercise rights of the majority were ignored in favor of a "positively wooden" application of the establishment clause, reinforced by the "resounding but fallacious fundamentalist rhetoric" so well criticized in the Stewart opinion in the Sherbert case.[18]

The rendition of these two decisions on the same day illustrates the peril in comfortably assuming that *Sherbert* guarantees the validity of federal aid to parochial schools. Rather, the fate of such aid will depend upon whether the Court follows the rigid and doctrinaire approach of the school prayer cases or the more rational technique of the Sherbert case. Given the tenacious adherence by a majority of the Court to abstractions, the constitutional future of aid to parochial schools is not unclouded.

Let us keep these implications of the Sherbert case in mind as we resume our discussion of the principal cases relevant to the constitutionality of achieving a public purpose by aiding church-related schools.

The Court in 1961 upheld various Sunday closing laws, although they conferred a benefit upon churches by making worshippers more readily available on Sundays, because the laws were "temporal statutes" with a valid secular public purpose.[19] Also, the Court held the non-religious purpose of the laws to be a sufficient justification for the indirect burden on the free exercise of their religion by those who do not observe Sunday as the Sabbath. Mr. Justice Stewart has asserted that this result is inconsistent with the ruling in *Sherbert v. Verner,* where the Court disallowed the imposition of a burden on the free exercise of the petitioner's religion.[20]

If we apply the public purpose criterion of Bradfield (1899), Cochran (1930), Everson (1947) and McGowan (1961), we can find justification for some forms of federal aid to church-related schools. This conclusion is reinforced by the decision in *Zorach v. Clauson,*[21] the 1952 case which upheld the New York released time program. Four years earlier, in *McCollum v. Board of Education,* the Court had nullified an Illinois released time plan where the religious instruction of the students was held on public school property.[22] In the New York plan approved in Zorach, the instruction was held off the public school premises, but the favorable decision may also have been based upon the absence of the compulsion which the Court found inherent in the McCollum stituation. Mr. Justice Douglas, for the Court in Zorach, sanctioned at least some forms of government cooperation with churches and religion:

> We are a religious people whose institutions presuppose a Supreme Being. . . . When the state encourages religious instruction or cooperates with religious authorities by adjusting the schedule of public events to sectarian needs, it follows the best of our traditions. For it then respects the religious nature of our people and accommodates the public service to their spiritual needs. To hold that it may not would be to find in the Constitution a requirement that the government show a callous indifference to religious groups. That would be preferring those who believe in no religion over those who do believe.[23]

Justice Douglas, in his concurring opinion in the 1962 Regents' Prayer case, said: "The Everson Case seems in retrospect to be out of line with the First Amendment."[24] Rather, it seems that the current views of Justice Douglas are out of line with the public purpose doctrine of the Bradfield, Cochran, Everson and McGowan cases, and the Zorach preference of church-state cooperation over hostility.

Two other cases are of interest on the aid question. In *Meyer v. Nebraska,*[25] in 1923, the Court held that a state law forbidding the teaching in any elementary school of any other than the English language was unconstitutional as an unreasonable interference with the natural right and duty of parents to give their children a suitable education, in this case a training in a foreign language. In *Pierce v. Society of Sisters,*[26] in 1925, the Court held that an Oregon statute requiring all children to attend public schools was unconstitutional as a violation of the right of private schools to exist and "the liberty of parents and guardians to direct the upbringing and education of children under their control."[27] The statute also violated the right of the children themselves to attend private schools. The Meyer and Pierce cases recognize the rights of parents and children to resort to private schools and the right of those schools to exist. These are rights which the government may not abolish or unreasonably curtail. These prior rights assume great importance in view of the likelihood that a massive program of federal aid which excluded church-related schools would drive many of those schools out of competition and into extinction. It can thus fairly be said that a program of aid which excluded parochial school students "because of their faith," in the words of the Everson and Sherbert decisions, would lay an unconstitutional burden upon the free exercise of religion by those children and their parents.

In summary, then, we can say that the possible extension of the school prayer decisions to invalidate aid to parochial schools would not only enthrone the abstraction at the expense of justice, but would also run counter to the best available precedents.

A PERSONAL RESERVATION

On the question of federal aid to church-related schools, its constitutionality and wisdom must be treated separately. The extension of federal grants or loans to such schools, to assist in their teaching of secular subjects, would probably not violate the First Amendment. Moreover, the exclusion of those schools from a program of federal aid limited only to public schools would probably violate the freedom of religious exercise of parochial school students and their parents. However, I am strongly opposed, on several grounds, to general federal aid to education, whether public or private. I wish to state that opposition to counter any possible construction of this chapter as an implicit endorsement of the wisdom of such federal aid.

Briefly, in my opinion, federal aid to public education is unnecessary because, as federal government statistics indicate, the states and local communities are adequately meeting their educational needs. Furthermore, a general federal subsidy of local schools would entail an unacceptable risk of burdensome federal administrative controls. The risk of federal control would be minimized it is true, in a program which merely allowed parents a credit against, or deduction from, their federal income tax for their educational expenditures. It could even be argued, also, that a private school which accepts a government subsidy, whether state or federal, assumes the constitutional restrictions incumbent upon the subsidizing government, including the obligations of the First Amendment.[28] It could result that religious exercises, religious preferences in admission policies, and similar sectarian practices of governmentally subsidized church-related schools would be as unconstitutional as if they were performed by the government itself. Church related schools, it is true, are in financial difficulty. However, instead of seeking relief from the federal government where that relief would be merely incidental to an unnecessary and cumbersome program of federal aid to public schools, churches ought to seek an appropriate remedy on the state and local levels, where the existence of the religious school systems directly benefits the general taxpayer by relieving the burden on public schools. In addition to the absence of clear constitutional authority for the federal government to intrude into the general educational field, the substantial indebtedness of that government argues persuasively against the creation of a new, expensive and unnecessary educational program.

The issue of whether there ought to be federal aid to education is a large one, and a detailed treatment is beyond the scope of this work. I offer these remarks, without supporting argument, merely to forestall any confusion here of the questions of constitutionality and wisdom.

V

1. Griswold, "Absolute Is In the Dark," 8 *Utah Law Review* 167, 168 (1963).
2. *Everson v. Board of Education,* 330 U.S. 1, 63 (1947).
3. Report, Prayers in Public Schools and Other Matters, Senate Committee on the Judiciary, (87th Cong., 2nd Sess.), 1962, 116.
4. Report, Prayers in Public Schools and Other Matters, Senate Committee on the Judiciary, (87th Cong., 2nd Sess.), 1962, 236–232.
5. 374 U.S. at 216.
6. 374 U.S. at 216.
7. 374 U.S. at 222.
8. 175 U.S. 291 (1899).
9. 281 U.S. 370 (1930).
10. 330 U.S. 1 (1947).
11. 330 U.S. at 15.
12. 330 U.S. at 16.
13. 374 U.S. 398 (1963).
14. 374 U.S. at 401.
15. 374 U.S. at 414.
16. 374 U.S. at 415.
17. 374 U.S. at 415–416.
18. 374 U.S. at 414, 416.
19. *McGowan v. Maryland,* 366 U.S. 420 (1961).
20. See 374 U.S. at 418, where Justice Stewart expressly said that *Braunfeld v. Brown,* one of the Sunday closing cases, should be overruled. See above, p. 13.
21. 343 U.S. 306 (1952).
22. *McCollum v. Board of Education,* 333 U.S. 203 (1948).
23. 343 U.S. at 313–314.
24. 370 U.S. at 443.
25. 262 U.S. 390 (1923).
26. 268 U.S. 510 (1925).
27. 268 U.S. at 533–534.
28. See, for example, *Burton v. Wilmington Parking Authority,* 365 U.S. 715 (1961), holding that a tenant operating a restaurant on state-owned property is bound by the Fourteenth Amendment in the same way as the state and cannot discriminate racially in its service of customers.

[T]he power to tax involves the power to destroy . . .

JOHN MARSHALL
Chief Justice of the United States
in McCulloch v. Maryland (1819)

VI

Effect on Tax Privileges of Religious Organizations

Religious organizations in this country are generally exempt from the payment of taxes on real property they own. They are exempt from payment of income taxes, and contributions to them are deductible from the donor's federal income tax. Mr. Justice Douglas, in the Regents' Prayer case, announced his opinion that these and other such benefits are unconstitutional, and he reiterated this view in the Schempp case.

As we have seen, the school prayer cases signal the acceptance by the Supreme Court of a dual prohibition against the state and federal governments—they may not conduct or sponsor a "religious exercise," and, to a newly uncertain extent, they may not finance religion or religious groups. Tax benefits, as obvious financial aids, are therefore called into question. We must inquire, then, whether the logic of the rulings will lead to a repudiation of those traditional aids to religion. Nor is this a minor issue. Indeed, it is the most important practical question involved in the school prayer controversy. The facts of contemporary life and taxation would prevent the continued effective operation of many religious denominations if they were now deprived of the general tax supports to which they have grown accustomed. Whatever may be said for the desirability of wholly private, voluntary support for religious groups, that ideal must be tempered by the reality that the tax system, especially on the federal level, operates to dry the springs of private charity through the confiscation of private resources. In the real world today, a withdrawal of the longstanding tax privileges of religious bodies would cause their rapid pauperization. Only the larger and more affluent could survive, and even as to these, survival would involve a curtailment of their activities, especially in education. The resulting diminution of total religious activity would be accompanied by a lessening of that diversity and private responsibility which are essential to a healthy, pluralistic society. If one desired to deal a crippling blow to organized religion in the United States, the withdrawal of existing tax privileges would be a most effective weapon.

Tax benefits have been extended lately to non-theistic religious bodies, such as the Ethical Culture Society. It could not be said, therefore, that religious tax privileges operate to favor only theistic religions. Rather, their invalidity would have to be rested upon a supposed inability of government to aid religion in general or all religious groups indiscriminately.

In neither of the school prayer cases did the opinion of the Court discuss the tax benefit problem. The Schempp Court, however, laid great stress upon its belief that the First Amendment goes further than to forbid only the preferential treatment of one or some religions. Instead, the Court in that case affirmed that the standard of "neutrality" is designed to prevent a situation where "official support of the State or Federal Government would be placed behind the tenets of one *or of all* orthodoxies" (Italics added).[1] The opinion, written by Mr. Justice Clark, quoted approvingly the following language from the dissenting opinions in the 1947 Everson school bus case:[2]

> There is no answer to the proposition . . . that the effect of the religious freedom Amendment to our Constitution was to take every form of propagation of religion out of the realm of things which could *directly or indirectly be made public business and thereby be supported in whole or in part at taxpayers' expense* . . . (Italics added).[3]

> The (First) Amendment's purpose was . . . to create a com-

plete and permanent separation of the spheres of religious activity and civil authority by *comprehensively forbidding every form of public aid or support for religion* (Italics added).[4]

The Schempp Court did, however, leave room for some sort of incidental aid to religion by stating the following test, which we discussed in Chapter V:

> The test may be stated as follows: what are the purpose and the primary effect of the enactment? If either is the advancement or inhibition of religion then the enactment exceeds the scope of legislative power as circumscribed by the Constitution. That is to say that to withstand the strictures of the Establishment Clause there must be a secular legislative purpose and a primary effect that neither advances nor inhibits religion.[5]

As with federal aid to education, it would be difficult to say that tax privileges do not have "a primary effect" that "advances" religion. Tax privileges, moreover, operate to assist directly the purely religious, non-commercial activities of churches, while most aid to education proposals limit the aid to the secular instruction performed by church-related schools. For this reason, their constitutionality cannot readily be affirmed by applying the public purpose doctrine of the Everson case, or the anti-discrimination rule of *Sherbert v. Verner,* both of which we discussed in Chapter V. Mr. Justice Brennan, in his concurring opinion in the Schempp case, attempted to save the day by justifying the tax privileges as nondiscriminatory provisions "which incidentally benefit churches and religious institutions along with many secular charities and nonprofit organizations."[6] Further, he said: "There is no indication that taxing authorities have used such benefits in any way to subsidize worship or foster belief in God."[7] Justice Brennan in that sentence appears to justify the tax privileges because he found they were not used with a *purpose* to foster religion. In that conclusion he is probably incorrect. The majority opinion in the Schempp case, moreover, said that an enactment would be invalid if its purpose *or a primary effect* were to aid religion.[8] Mr. Justice Brennan seems to overlook the obvious effect of the tax privileges. Further, he justifies them as merely a sharing by the religious organizations, "in spite of rather than because of their religious character,"[9] in general tax benefits designed to advance secular educational and charitable ends. But in that same opinion, Mr. Justice Brennan drew from his interpretation of previous cases a conclusion "that government may not employ religious means to serve secular interests, however legitimate they may be, at least without the clearest demonstration that nonreligious means will not suffice.[10] If the objective of the tax exemption is really to promote charitable, educational and other worthwhile secular ends, even the Brennan opinion would allow a finding that nonreligious means would suffice for the attainment of those purely secular ends and that therefore the religious means may not be employed. It is conceivable that this Court could find there was not "the clearest demonstration" that tax benefits to nonreligious charities would not serve those purely secular ends as well as would benefits to religious societies.

Mrs. Madalyn Murray, the militant atheist who was the plaintiff in the Baltimore Bible-reading case, decided by the Supreme Court in the Schempp opinion in 1963, has already started lawsuits in several states to invalidate the tax privileges of religious organizations.

The Supreme Court, in rendering a decision, decides only the issue before it. Neither of the school prayer decisions, therefore, decided the tax question. We cannot say with certainty, then, what will be the outcome when that issue is squarely presented to the Court. It is a fair conclusion, however, that there is nothing in those decisions to prevent the invalidation of the tax privileges, since those privileges operate directly to subsidize the purely religious activities of churches. We can even go further and say that the logic of the various opinions makes that result a probability. Especially is this so in view of the Court's uncritical devotion to abstractions and its adherence to the extravagant language of its own prior decisions. The record does not justify a confident assumption that, on this already pending and most critical issue, the Court will resist the demands of those who relentlessly seek to carry the Court's own logic to this further conclusion. There are those who belittle predictions that tax privileges will be abolished, by pointing to the fact that the Court has decided only the issues of the school prayers themselves and has made no binding judgment on the tax question. But those same apologists were telling us not long ago that *Engel v. Vitale* was nothing to worry about because all the Court decided was that the state could not *compose* a Regents' Prayer. The decision, we were told by the pundits, had nothing to do with any other prayers or any other elements of religion in public life.

I frankly expect these tax privileges to be invalidated in the early course of events, unless the present trend of decision is checked. Regrettably, restraint will have to be effected by Congress or by the people acting through the process of constitutional amendment, because the notion of judicial self-restraint has fallen out of favor within the Court itself. Unless such a check is placed upon the Court, we may fairly expect the abolition of all tax privileges accorded to the religious activities of religious organization. In which event, there will be "separation of church and state," but few churches.

VI

1. 374 U.S. at 222.
2. 374 U.S. at 216, 217.
3. Dissenting opinion of Mr. Justice Jackson in *Everson v. Board of Education,* 330 U.S. 1, 26 (1947).
4. Dissenting opinion of Mr. Justice Rutledge, joined by Justices Frankfurter, Jackson and Burton, in *Everson v. Board of Education,* 330 U.S. 1, 31–32 (1947).
5. 374 U.S. at 222.
6. 374 U.S. at 301.
7. 374 U.S. at 301.
8. 374 U.S. at 222.
9. 374 U.S. at 301.
10. 374 U.S. at 265.

He hoped, therefore, the amendment would be made in such a way as to secure the rights of conscience, and a free exercise of the rights of religion, but not to patronise those who professed no religion at all.

REPRESENTATIVE BENJAMIN HUNTINGTON
of Connecticut, as quoted in
the Annals of the First Congress

VII

Other Undesirable Results of School Prayer Decisions

SHARPENING OF RELIGIOUS BITTERNESS

Already, the school prayer decisions have brought in their train a rise in bitterness among, and even within, religious denominations. We have already noted the suspicion in some quarters that the Roman Catholic clergy are motivated in their attacks upon the decisions by a lurking desire for federal aid. The circumstance that units of some minority religious groups have led the fight against public prayer has introduced an element of recrimination on that score also. The same article from the *Baptist Press* that was quoted earlier concerning the Catholic clergy, continued in the following vein:

> Nobody will admit it but resentment against Jews, free-thinkers, Unitarians, and atheists goes a long way to explain the negative reaction of many people against the Supreme Court. While it is true, and perhaps unfortunate, that many of the cases involving religious liberty have been initiated by minority and unpopular groups, it is not true that these groups are imposing their views on the American People.
>
> Basic policies of American life should be decided on principle. Reactions to decisions should be made on the basis of right and wrong rather than on prejudice.[1]

With the substantive reasoning of most of that passage all right-minded persons would agree. Prejudice ought not to play a part in the resolution of critical national questions. Unfortunately, though, the first sentence of the quotation is symptomatic of a too-prevalent belief that, because different religious groups have polarized on opposite sides of the prayer question, their positions are determined in substantial part by dislike of their opponents rather than by a sober judgment on the merits on the issue. Let us make it clear that men of good faith are found on both sides of this question and that there is no occasion here for a ready imputation of baser motives to one's antagonists. This problem of preserving good will was highlighted by an editorial in *America* magazine, a Jesuit publication, on September 1, 1962, entitled, "To Our Jewish Friends," in which the editors expressed their view that certain of the Jewish service organizations, notably the American Jewish Congress, the Union of American Hebrew Congregations and the Central Conference of American Rabbis, were so vocal in their insistence upon further implementation of the *Engel v. Vitale* decision that "there have been disturbing hints of heightened anti-Semitic feeling." The editors urged "responsible Jewish spokesmen" to make it plain that "the all-out campaign to secularize the public schools and public life from top to bottom, as that campaign is conceived and implemented by Mr. Pfeffer[2] and a few Jewish organizations, does *not* genuinely represent the ideas of the whole Jewish community." The editorial concluded:

> The time has come for these fellow citizens of ours to decide among themselves precisely what they conceive to be the final objective of the Jewish community in the United States—in a word, what bargain they are willing to strike as one of the minorities in a pluralistic society. When court victories produce only a harvest of fear and distrust, will it all have been worth-while?

One interesting result of this effort to forestall religious strife was that it engendered, on the one hand, a response from many Jewish leaders who took issue with the secularistic stance of some vocal Jewish organizations, but on the other hand, a series of strident denunciations by representatives of those very groups, who intimated that the editors of *America* were themselves stirring up anti-semitism by "warning" American Jews to forego the assertion of their constitutional rights.

Two lessons can be drawn from the episode. One is that great caution must be exercised in concluding that official or self-appointed spokesmen for the position of any faith, whether the editors of *America* or the leaders of the American Jewish Congress, necessarily represent the thinking of all or most of the members of their sects when they speak on public matters. The second is that there is no profit, and great danger, in the polarization of the school prayer controversy into an inter-faith conflict. Leo Pfeffer is a gentleman of integrity and dedication to the Constitution, as are the editors of *America.* It is indicative of the extent to which the school prayer decisions have touched a sensitive nerve in American life, and have offended the instinct and conviction of a majority of the people, that the controversy threatens in some quarters to become an interreligious one. The dialogue among men of good will is in danger of interruption. Perhaps nothing demonstrates more clearly the wisdom of judicial restraint.

INVALIDATION OF MISCELLANEOUS RELIGIOUS PRACTICES

It is possible to envision a startling series of public religious observances which are imperilled by the school prayer decisions. A good place to begin is the concurring opinion of Mr. Justice Douglas in *Engel v. Vitale:*

> The point for decision is whether the Government can constitutionally finance a religious exercise. Our system at the federal and state levels is presently honeycombed with such financing. Nevertheless, I think it is an unconstitutional undertaking whatever form it takes.[3]

Mr. Justice Douglas then enumerated in a footnote the types of "financing" he believes to be unconstitutional:

> There are many "aids" to religion in this country at all levels of government. To mention but a few at the federal level, one might begin by observing that the very First Congress which wrote the First Amendment provided for chaplains in both Houses and in the armed services. There is compulsory chapel at the service academies, and religious services are

> held in federal hospitals and prisons. The President issues religious proclamations. The Bible is used for the administration of oaths. N.Y.A. and W.P.A. funds were available to parochial schools during the depression. Veterans receiving money under the "G.I." Bill of 1944 could attend denominational schools, to which payments were made directly by the government. During World War II, federal money was contributed to denominational schools for the training of nurses. The benefits of the National School Lunch Act are available to students in private as well as public schools. The Hospital Survey and Construction Act of 1946 specifically made money available to non-public hospitals. The slogan "In God We Trust" is used by the Treasury Department, and Congress recently added God to the pledge of allegiance. There is Bible-reading in the schools of the District of Columbia, and religious instruction is given in the District's National Training School for Boys. Religious organizations are exempt from the federal income tax and are granted postal privileges. Up to defined limits—15 per cent of the adjusted gross income of individuals and 5 per cent of the net income of corporations—contributions to religious organizations are deductible for federal income tax purposes. There are no limits to the deductibility of gifts and bequests to religious institutions made under the federal gift and estate tax laws. This list of federal "aids" could easily be expanded and of course there is a long list in each state. Fellman, *The Limits of Freedom* (1959), pp. 40–41.[4]

These very practices, condemned as unconstitutional in the Douglas dictum, are in reality but manifestations of the underlying, and continuing, national tradition that, in the words of Justice Douglas himself: "We are a religious people whose institutions presuppose a Supreme Being."[5] To affirm that tradition in a generality, while stifling the specific manifestations through which it is expressed and maintained as a living thing, is symptomatic of a regrettable judicial schizophrenia. It would be a mistake, though, to dwell upon the extreme position of Justice Douglas and neglect the more important fact that he is merely articulating the logical consequences of the wayward theories endorsed by the majority of the Justices. Those members of the Court who hold back from a thorough implementation of the reigning absolutist ideas are perhaps even more in error than Justice Douglas.

For he, at least, is logical in the application of the mistaken premises.

The Douglas position is not avowed by any other member of the Court. Mr. Justice Clark, speaking for the Court in the Schempp case, mentioned various religious manifestations in American public life, such as chaplains and prayers in legislative halls, and the supplication, "So help me God," in oaths of office, but proclaimed no intention to strike them down. And Justices Goldberg and Harlan cautioned in general terms against the adoption of "a brooding and pervasive devotion to the secular and a passive, or even active, hostility to the religious." Mr. Justice Black, in the Regents' Prayer case, took pains to state that nothing in the decision was inconsistent with "patriotic or ceremonial" manifestations of belief in God in our public life. We cannot say, then, that the Court majority is knowingly embarked upon a crusade to eradicate every vestige of theistic belief from our public life. Rather, the inquiry should be whether the Court is likely to find itself trapped by its own reasoning and gratuitous dicta and impelled to sanction extreme results rather than repudiate the theoretical foundations of the school prayer decisions.

In Chapter V, we discussed the problems raised by government financial aid to religion. Akin to that is the question of chaplains, and we have noted, at page 7, that government employment of chaplains can no longer be considered secure from attack. The New Jersey division of the American Civil Liberties Union has already challenged the employment of chaplains in the military services.[6] In this chapter, however, we are considering primarily those governmental encouragements of religion which do not entail a substantial appropriation of money, and which are therefore attacked on other, non-financial grounds.

The Schempp decision indicates that a state or federal law will be invalidated if it entails governmental conduct or sponsorship of a "religious exercise"[7] or if it has a purpose or a primary effect that "advances" or "inhibits" religion.[8] Some of the items in the Douglas catalogue can be called religious exercises, such as Presidential religious proclamations and the imprinting on money of the national motto, "In God We Trust." There are two ways to preserve such exercises from invalidation. One is to say they are "de minimis," that is, too trifling to merit the notice of the law. This is hardly tenable, however, because these observances have a way of taking on considerable symbolic importance. Mr. Justice Brennan, in the Schempp case, expressly denied that the motto was "de minimis." Instead, he sought to preserve it from extinction by resorting to the vague statement: "The truth is that we have simply interwoven the motto so deeply into the fabric of our civil polity that its present use may well not present that type of involvement which the First Amendment prohibits."[9] It is curious that the same reasoning was not applied to Bible reading and the recital of the Lord's Prayer in public schools, which practices have a longer history on a widespread scale, and an earlier statutory acknowledgment, than the national motto.

The second way to uphold such public religious observances is to say that they have lost their meaning. The Court in the Schempp case contented itself with a general acknowledgment that such public religious manifestations do exist, and that they reflect "a religious people," but it went no further.[10] Mr. Justice Brennan, however, rested squarely on this reasoning. Thus he followed his above statement about the "interwoven" motto with the following observation, to which we have already referred:[11]

> This general principle might also serve to insulate the various *patriotic* exercises and activities used in the public schools and elsewhere which, whatever may have been their origins, *no longer have a religious purpose or meaning.* The reference to divinity in the revised pledge of allegiance, for example, may merely recognize the historical fact that our Nation *was believed to have been founded "under God."* Thus reciting the pledge may be no more of a religious exercise than the reading aloud of Lincoln's Gettysburg Address, which contains an allusion to the same histroical fact (Italics added).[12]

Mr. Justice Brennan's implication, that President Lincoln concurred in the sort of non-believing historical commemoration which the Brennan opinion approves, does not square with the forthright national and personal avowals of faith contained in Lincoln's 1863 proclamation of a day of national prayer, reproduced in *Appendix D.* It will come as a surprise to the Congress to learn that when, in 1954 and 1956, it inserted "under God" in the pledge of allegiance, and adopted "In God We Trust" as the national motto, it was doing so as a mere commemoration of the historical fact that, in the early days, the founders of the Republic, deprived of the cultural resources of the twentieth century, actually believed they were founding a nation "under God" and actually put their trust in Him. On the contrary, the House Committee on the Judiciary, when it recommended the insertion of "under God," in the pledge, emphatically asserted, in the present tense, "the dependence of our people and our Government upon the moral directions of the Creator."[13]

This apparent requirement, that religious manifestations in public life may be retained only if they are not to be believed, was supported by a footnote in *Engel v. Vitale,* in which Mr. Justice Black, for the Court, said:

> There is of course nothing in the decision reached here that is inconsistent with the fact that school children and others are officially encouraged to *express love for our country* by reciting historical documents such as the Declaration of Independence which contain references to the Deity or by singing officially espoused anthems which include the composer's professions of faith in a Supreme Being, or with the fact that there are many manifestations in our public life of belief in God. *Such patriotic or ceremonial occasions* bear no true resemblance to the unquestioned religious exercise that the State of New York has sponsored in this instance (Italics added).[14]

This standard would lead one to conclude that if the national motto, "In God We Trust," were designed to express love for God as well as love for our country, it would thereby become a forbidden religious exercise.

It appears that Mr. Justice Brennan has supplied the key the Court is likely to use to decide if an exercise is "religious" or merely a harmless "patriotic or ceremonial" one. That is, if it is to be taken seriously, it is therefore at least in part a "religious exercise," and as such it is prohibited by the First Amendment. Only if it is a mere affirmation of the historical fact that the founders believed in the overlordship of God, or that some Americans now so believe, and only if it scrupulously avoids any affirmation of the truth or falsity of that belief in God, can the observance be insulated from constitutional attack.

There are many observances in public life which could be termed "religious exercises." The national motto, by Act of Congress, is, "In God We Trust." The same inscription is over the south door of the United States Senate, and over the east door we read, "God smiles on this undertaking." Chief Justice Warren has voiced his disapproval of a pending Congressional bill to inscribe "In God We Trust" above the bench of the Supreme Court.[15] The Chief Justice observed, in a letter to the architect of the Capitol, that:

> The Supreme Court Building and particularly the courtroom were designed by outstanding architects and were decorated with an eye to beauty and symmetry consistent with the purpose for which the building was to be devoted. It is believed that ornamentation other than that provided in the original plans would detract from the total concept of the building. On other occasions, people have suggested patriotic and religious inscriptions for the courtroom, but it has always been the view of the members of our Court then sitting that no changes in the decor of the courtroom should be made. This has been true regardless of the significance of the language or its relevance to patriotic or religious sentiment. I believe that the suggestion contained in these bills should be no exception to our previous views.

Democratic Congressman Robert T. Ashmore of South Carolina replied:

> the language and tone of this letter indicate much more than a concern for "beauty and symmetry." The tone is most indicative that the Supreme Court would be made painfully aware of the fact that there is an authority higher than that of the Supreme Court of these United States.[16]

The oaths in our courts include the words, "So help me, God," as do the oaths of military personnel. Daily sessions of the Senate and House of Representatives are opened with prayer. Each session of the Supreme Court is opened with the supplication, "God save the United States and this Honorable Court." On naval vessels, time-honored custom dictates the flying of the church flag during religious services. State laws confer legal validity upon marriages performed by clergymen pursuant to church ritual, a most important practical benefit to churches. Incidentally, Mr. Justice Douglas, in the Schempp case, commented that in the sort of establishment of religion which is prohibited by the First Amendment, "church law usually governs such matters as baptism, *marriage,* divorce and separation. . . ." (Italics added.)[17] The national anthem, adopted by Act of Congress in 1931, contains the following invocation in its final stanza:

> Blest with victory and peace, may the heav'n rescued land
> Praise the Pow'r that hath made and preserved us a nation!
> Then conquer we must, when our cause it is just;
> And this be our motto: "In God is our trust."[18]

The New York State Commissioner of Education, applying *Engel v. Vitale,* has already prohibited the devotional use of this stanza in public schools. The same fate has befallen a similar use of the hymn, "America," the last stanza of which proclaims:

> Our fathers' God, to Thee
> Author of Liberty
> To Thee we sing,
> Long may our land be bright,
> With Freedom's holy light,
> Protect us by Thy might
> Great God, our King.

Christmas, Easter and Chanukah observances in schools or otherwise publicly sponsored would surely be considered religious exercises. On the same day it decided the Schempp case, June 17, 1963, the Supreme Court sent back to the Supreme Court of Florida, "for further consideration in light of" the Schempp ruling, a case in which the Florida court upheld, in addition to Bible reading and the Lord's Prayer, the singing of religious hymns and the holding of baccalaureate exercises in public schools.[19] Mr. Justice Brennan, in his opinion which attempted to avoid the extreme implications of the Schempp decision, was constrained to indicate that "the regular use of public school property for religious activities," such as the erection of a Nativity scene, may be unconstitutional.[20] In fact, Mr. Justice Brennan's assertion "that morning devotional exercises *in any form* are constitutionally invalid"[21] (Italics added), compels the conclusion that school children may not even think a prayer unless the period of silent thought is called something other than "devotional."

The Los Angeles branch of the American Civil Liberties Union instituted suit, promptly after the Schempp decision, to erase the words "under God" from the pledge of allegiance. Similar cases are pending in the courts of other states. The issue ultimately will reach the Supreme Court, as probably will others challenging various religious elements in public life. It is likely that the Supreme Court will uphold the pledge, or any of the other practices in question, only if it finds that the acknowledgment of God is not to be taken seriously. This would be in keeping with the Court's apparent mandate that government must maintain a perpetual suspension of judgment on the question of God's existence and, indeed, on all questions of God. It would offer another convincing proof that the Court, in its search for a "neutrality" impossible of attainment, has truly established agnosticism as the official public religion of these United States. In a way, it would be preferable for the Court to strike down the motto, the national anthem and the rest, rather than leave their words intact under the stipulation that they are not to be believed. In the one case, a removal of the theistic words would establish agnosticism. But in the other case, their continuance as things to be seen but not believed, would not only enshrine agnosticism, but would convict the government of hypocrisy as well. And so we see the mischief that follows in the train of the Court's repudiation of the basic theistic postulates upon which our nation is grounded.

The objection of Mr. Justice Douglas to the various religious features of public life is not simply to their character as religious exercises (although he would object to that, as well), but principally to the fact that public funds, however slight, are used in their conduct. If Mr. Justice Douglas could find, as he did, a significant use of public funds in the conduct of Bible reading or the Lord's Prayer in public schools, he would certainly find it in all the ceremonial practices we have mentioned in this section. It is doubtful, however, that a majority of the Court would follow suit and rely upon the involvement of public funds to invalidate those observances. In most cases, the expenditure, if any, is so slight, as to be detectable only to the grimly determined abstractionist. Unlike the more substantial financial aids to religion, it is probable that if the various ceremonial manifestations of belief in God are to be invalidated, it will be because they are, in the Court's opinion, "religious exercises," and therefore beyond the power of government to conduct or sponsor. It is not the purpose here to dramatize the point, but it does seem that, unless the trend of the school prayer decisions is checked, many of the religious elements of public life enumerated in this section and in Chapter III, will be constitutionally forbidden. Perhaps it is not fantastic to suppose that the display in a public building of the picture of General Washington on his knees at Valley Forge, might constitute a "law respecting an establishment of religion, or prohibiting the free exercise thereof." A crusading secular litigator may even one day discover that the Pearl Harbor memorial plaque reads: "May God make His face to shine on them in lasting peace."

VII

1. Garrett, "The Storm in The Capitol," *Baptist Press,* July 12, 1962.
2. Mr. Leo Pfeffer, General Counsel of the American Jewish Congress.
3. 370 U.S. at 437.
4. 370 U.S. at 437.
5. *Zorach v. Clauson,* 343 U.S. 306, 313 (1952).
6. *New York Times,* September 15, 1963.
7. 374 U.S. at 224.
8. 374 U.S. at 222.
9. 374 U.S. at 303.
10. 374 U.S. at 213.
11. See above, p. 19.
12. 374 U.S. at 303–304.
13. Report No. 1693, 83rd Cong., 2nd Sess.
14. 370 U.S. at 435.
15. H.R. 7252 (88th Cong., 1st Sess.).
16. Congressional Record, Nov. 12, 1963, p. 20539.
17. 374 U.S. at 227.
18. See above, p. 55
19. *Chamberlin v. Dade County Board of Public Instruction,* 374 U.S.

487 (1963). On its rehearing of the case, the Florida Supreme Court refused to order the discontinuance of Bible reading and the recitation of the Lord's Prayer. The Court said that if these practices are to be denied to the children of Florida, it will have to be done by order of the Supreme Court of the United States, not the Florida Court. 160 So. 2d 97 (1964); *New York Times,* January 30, 1964.

20. 374 U.S. at 298.
21. 374 U.S. at 301.

As the safety and prosperity of nations ultimately and essentially depend on the protection and the blessing of Almighty God, and the national acknowledgment of this truth is not only an indispensable duty which the people owe to Him, but a duty whose natural influence is favorable to the promotion of that morality and piety without which social happiness can not exist nor the blessings of a free government be enjoyed . . .

PRESIDENT JOHN ADAMS
Proclamation of a day of national humiliation, fasting and prayer. 1798

VIII

Practical Benefits from Governmental Promotion of Recognition of God

Much of the school prayer debate has naturally centered upon the constitutionality of the practices in question, rather than their wisdom. However, the effort to determine whether government has power, under First Amendment standards, to promote the recognition of God, ought not to eclipse the logically subordinate but practically equal inquiry into the effect of such promotion upon the common good. It is not enough for proponents of public prayer to assert its legal constitutionality, any more than it fully served the cause of total abstinence in the 1920's to recite the language of the Eighteenth Amendment. If the public acknowledgment of God is to endure as a part of the American way of life, its capacity to do so will spring from a conviction of the people that it serves the general welfare.

There are several civic purposes served by government-sponsored prayer. One is the inculcation of morality, virtue and self-discipline in the citizens, irrespective of sectarian differences among theistic religions on doctrinal points. The Pennsylvania statute which ratified the practice of Bible reading in that state recognized that, "it is in the interest of good moral training, of a life of honorable thought and of good citizenship, that the public school children should have lessons of morality brought to their attention during their school days."[1] That this training in morality is supplementary to the training received at home was recognized by the Board of Regents of the State of New York in its 1951 Statement of Belief, recommending that the Regent's Prayer be included in the school program:

> We believe that thus the school will fulfill its high function of supplementing the training of the home, ever intensifying in the child that love for God, for parents and for home which is the mark of true character training and the sure guarantee of a country's welfare.

It can hardly be disputed that this nation would benefit from a strengthening of individual morality, virtue and self-discipline. Indeed, authoritative voices are heard to say that improvement here is an urgent need. Mr. J. Edgar Hoover, Director of the Federal Bureau of Investigation, put it this way in his address on October 9, 1962, to the national convention of the American Legion:

> What has happened to the time-honored precepts of hard work and fair play which influenced the American scene during the all-important formative years of this great Republic? Where is the faith in God which fortified us through our past trials? Have our national pride, our moral conscience, our sensitivity to filth and degradation, grown so weak that they no longer react to assaults upon our proud heritage of freedom?
>
> Crime and subversion are formidable problems in the United States today because, *and only because,* there is a dangerous flaw in our Nation's moral armor. Self-indulgence—the principle of pleasure before duty—is practiced across the length and breadth of the land. It is undermining those attributes of personal responsibility and self-discipline which are essential to our national survival. It is creating citizens who reach maturity with a warped sense of values and an undeveloped conscience.

In recent decades the schools of America have retreated from the unapologetic inculcation of love for God and country. Perhaps coincidentally, the educational philosophy of permissiveness gained supremacy during the same period. Today we are confronted with juvenile disciplinary problems of unprecedented magnitude. The tiny seed of pragmatic doubt sown in the 1920's has borne bitter fruit in a generation of students, too many of whom are indolent under instruction, docile under indoctrination, rebellious under correction and scornful under exposure to principle in the slightest degree. As Dr. Max Rafferty, Superintendent of Public Instruction of the State of California phrased it, in our schools today the ideal of the gentleman is too often giving way to "The Cult of the Slob." In too many places, "the triumphant Slob" reigns supreme. It is fair to say that the restoration and advancement of character will be furthered by teaching our children that there is indeed a "law of Nature and of Nature's God," which enjoins upon them a rejection of vagrant self-indulgence in favor of an ordered pursuit of a higher good.

Opponents of publicly-sponsored prayer sometimes ground their position on a desire to achieve a "truce" among "hostile religious sects."[2] The inclusion of religious invocations on public occasions, they say, is divisive and destructive of tolerant understanding. In fact, however, understanding and toleration are more likely to be impeded by a rigid excision of all religious references from public life. An official position which implies that religious beliefs are so fragile that the state cannot even invoke the name of God without imperiling some of them, threatens to engender in the citizen a jealously proprietary attitude toward his own particular creed. The policy of religious exclusion can only serve to impede the free and easy interchange of ideas among denominations—an interchange which is the best guarantee of genuine religious brotherhood. The concept of tolerance, it must be remembered, requires that the tolerant person entertain a basic belief of his own. When others deviate from your own beliefs, you can tolerate their disagreement. But you cannot truly be tolerant unless you have a belief of your own to serve as a bench mark for the measurement of others. Webster's New International Dictionary defines tolerance as:

> The act, practice, or habit of tolerating; the quality of being tolerant; specif., the disposition to tolerate, or allow the existence of, beliefs, practices or habits *differing from one's own;* now often, freedom from bigotry; sympathetic understanding of others' beliefs, etc., without acceptance of them . . . (Italics added).

To be tolerant of the beliefs of others, therefore, a person must entertain a fixed belief of his own—for example, in the existence and providence of God. The same rule would seem to apply to governments and societies. We all desire the government and society to be tolerant in matters of religion. But if the basic belief officially adopted by that government or society is the agnostic position that we cannot know whether there is a God, we can call it tolerance only if we acknowledge that the government has adopted this agnostic position as a basic belief, an orthodoxy if you please, of its own. As between theistic and non-theistic religions, we have seen that the government cannot realistically be neutral. So also, it cannot be truly tolerant in matters of religion without affirming one or the other basic belief as true. This is a matter of some importance, for the militant secularizers often raise the banner of tolerance without acknowledging that what they would achieve would be not neutrality among sects, but a replacement of the traditional communal recognition of God by an official agnosticism.

Apart from the definitional problem, common sense tells us that inter-faith understanding can best be promoted when government frankly recognizes God. Dean Erwin N. Griswold of Harvard Law School said it this way in a passage worth quoting at length:

> Let us consider the Jewish child, or the Catholic child, or the nonbeliever, or the Congregationalist, or the Quaker. He, either alone, or with a few or many others of his views, attends a public school, whose School District, by local action, has prescribed the Regents' Prayer. When the prayer is recited, if this child or his parents feel that he cannot participate, he may stand or sit, in respectful attention, while the other children take part in the ceremony. Or he may leave the room. It is said that this is bad, because it sets him apart from other children. It is even said that there is an element of compulsion in this—what the Supreme Court has called an "indirect coercive pressure upon religious minorities to conform." But is this the way it should be looked at? The child of a nonconforming or minority group is, to be sure, different in his beliefs. That is what it means to be a member of a minority. Is it not desirable, and educational, for him to learn and observe this, in the atmosphere of the school—

> not so much that he is different, as that other children are different from him? And is it not desirable that, at the same time, he experiences and learns the fact that his difference is tolerated and accepted? No compulsion is put upon him. He need not participate. But he, too, has the opportunity to be tolerant. He allows the majority of the group to follow their own tradition, perhaps coming to understand and to respect what they feel is significant to them.
>
> Is this not a useful and valuable and educational and, indeed, a spiritual experience for the children of what I have called the majority group? They experience the values of their own culture; but they also see that there are others who do not accept those values, and that they are wholly tolerated in their nonacceptance. Learning tolerance for other persons, no matter how different, and respect for their beliefs, may be an important part of American education, and wholly consistent with the First Amendment. I hazard the thought that no one would think otherwise were it not for parents who take an absolutist approach to the problem, perhaps encouraged by the absolutist expressions of Justices of the Supreme Court, on and off the bench.[3]

The advancement of inter-faith understanding, then, may be said to be another purpose of governmental promotion of the recognition of God.

It is sometimes asserted that believers in God betray the weakness and insecurity of their own faith when they call upon the public school and government to advance it for them. If they really strongly believed, it is said, they would rely upon their own spiritual resources and would not seek to enlist the government to reassure them by inserting professions of theistic belief into public ceremonies. But can it not more truly be said that those who object to governmental recognition of God must be very weak in their own convictions, if they feel they would be threatened by the mere inclusion in public events of acknowledgments of God in which their participation is not required? In fact, the argument for governmental promotion of the recognition of God stems not from any latent insecurities of the believers, but rather from a realization of the fitness, and indeed necessity, of a public awareness that all, including the state, are subject to a higher law.

A central purpose of governmental acknowledgment of God is the promotion of a recognition by the citizens that there is a standard of right and wrong higher than the state. In the words of Episcopal Bishop James A. Pike, the government ought to promote "a recognition of dependence upon Almighty God and of the fact that He is the highest reality and not the state." The child who routinely sees the agents of the government, be they teachers or presidents, affirm the existence and supremacy of God and His law over all, is less likely to follow the demagogue who asserts for the state, and for himself as its oracle, the final power to ordain what is right and wrong in a matter of public or private morality. Moreover, an inculcation of mere ethical values without reference to their divine source cannot serve this purpose as well as an assertion of the supremacy of an unchanging lawgiver. For if ethical precepts arise from some non-divine source, such as the Constitution, a consensus or a social contract, then they can be subject to change or disregard by a totalitarian state or as well by a modern democracy enjoying the assent of a majority of its citizens.

In German legal theory in the first half of this century, there prevailed a concept called "Rechtspositivismus, the view that any law, however outrageous from the standpoint of moral law and natural right, has full validity and must be implemented."[4] It cannot be proven empirically, but one can well suspect that a child schooled in that philosophy could shrug his shoulders at rumors of gas ovens at Dachau—all operated pursuant to duly promulgated law or decree. In such atmosphere an Eichmann can flourish, or a Castro or a Khrushchev. On the contrary, a citizen reared on the precept, taught by the state itself, that even the state is subject to the moral law of God, can more readily resist the entrenchment of a regime at war with the obvious dictates of that higher law. If we are to preserve the limited government that is the hallmark of American constitutionalism, we can hardly disregard the lesson of history that the best assurance against tyranny is a citizenry devoted to ultimate values transcending the changing will of the state. On Thomas Jefferson's Memorial, there is inscribed his questioning warning: "God Who gave us life gave us liberty. Can the liberties of a nation be secure when we have removed a conviction that these liberties are the gift of God?"

VIII

1. Act of May 20, 1913, P.L. 226.
2. See Cahn, "On Government and Prayer," 37 *N.Y. Univ. L. Rev.* 981, 983 (1962), for a presentation of this argument by a constructive defender of the school prayer decisions.
3. Griswold, "Absolute Is In the Dark," 8 *Utah L. Rev.* 167, 177 (1963).
4. Chamberlin, "Germany's Former Nazi Judges," *Modern Age,* Winter, 1962–1963, 33, 34.

On every question of construction, carry ourselves back to the time when the Constitution was adopted, recollect the spirit manifested in the debates, and instead of trying what meaning may be squeezed out of the text, or invented against it, conform to the probable one in which it was passed.

THOMAS JEFFERSON
in 1823

IX

Toward a Solution: Judicial Self-restraint

We have examined the school prayer decisions, the inaccuracy of their historical foundation, the absurdity of their posture of neutrality, and the undesirable consequences of their continued ascendancy. It now remains to canvass the possible remedies for the problems the rulings have created. Hopefully, we seek a solution which can preserve the American tradition of freedom of religion encouraged, but not encumbered, by a limited, constitutional government. The decisions were the product of judicial license, an abandonment of the healthful canons of judicial self-restraint. The first remedy, then, would ideally be a revival of that self-restraint, a wholesome timidity in the judiciary, born of a realization that not all human problems are soluble by a central decree, even when that decree is couched in the learned forms of constitutional adjudication. This remedy necessarily demands a reformation by the Court itself. It requires an extraordinary optimism to envision that reformation, but we ought nevertheless to explore the constructive ways in which the change of heart could be effected.

STANDING TO SUE

There was no need for the Supreme Court to decide the school prayer cases at all. With full propriety, the Court could have found that the complainants lacked "standing" to compel adjudication of their grievances. In order to challenge, in a federal court, the constitutionality of a state or federal law, a person must have more than the money to pay a lawyer. He must be affected by the law he attacks in a way that is different from its effect upon his fellow-citizens in general. In short, he must have a peculiar, personal interest in the law which he seeks to invalidate. This means that while many citizens may object to a law, and desire its repeal or invalidation, only a comparatively few persons will be sufficiently affected by the law to ask in a lawsuit that a federal court declare it unconstitutional. We say that those who have such a sufficient interest have "standing to sue." The doctrine of standing is reasonable and useful. If great constitutional questions could be brought to the highest court by persons affected only incidentally or not at all by the practice in question, there could be an unwieldy number of such cases before the Court. Moreover, there would often be lacking the clarity of presentation which is born only of the sharply conflicting contentions of personally interested adversaries. For these reasons, the Supreme Court in 1923 decided, in the case of *Frothingham v. Mellon,* that a federal taxpayer has no right, from his mere status as a taxpayer, to challenge the constitutionality of a federal appropriation.[1] Therefore, Mrs. Harriet A. Frothingham, a Boston taxpayer, could not sue in a federal court to prevent Secretary of the Treasury Mellon from spending money which Congress had appropriated to carry out the federal Maternity Act of 1921. The Act provided a system of federal grants, administered through state agencies, designed to reduce maternal and infant mortality. Mrs. Frothingham contended that the Maternity Act was an unconstitutional invasion by the federal government of an area reserved by the Constitution to the states. However, she was affected by the Act only as a taxpayer, in that some indeterminate portion of her federal tax payment was used for the purpose of implementing the Act. This interest she shared in common with all taxpayers and the Court found it was too remote and infinitesimal. If Mrs. Frothingham's suit were sustained, any taxpayer, without limitation, could sue in a federal court to invalidate any statute and the Court felt this involved too great a risk of excessive litigation:

> The administration of any statute, likely to produce additional taxation to be imposed upon a vast number of taxpayers, the extent of whose several liability is indefinite and constantly changing, is essentially a matter of public and not of individual concern. If one taxpayer may champion and litigate such a cause, then every other taxpayer may do the same, not only in respect of the statute here under review but also in respect of every other appropriation act and statute whose administration requires the outlay of public money, and whose validity may be questioned. The bare suggestion of such a result, with its attendant inconveniences, goes far to sustain the conclusion which we have reached, that a suit of this character cannot be maintained.[2]

In First Amendment religion cases, the doctrine of standing developed along two lines. There are two clauses of the Amendment which deal with religion. The first prevents the enactment of any "law respecting an establishment of religion" and the second guards against a law "prohibiting the free exercise" of religion. Different requirements of "standing" were applied to these two clauses by the Supreme Court. Thus it was held that a person could not sue to strike down a state or federal law as a violation of the "establishment" clause of the First Amendment unless he could show either that he suffered an economic injury from the offending law —an injury of a different kind from that suffered by taxpayers in general through the expenditure of their tax funds— or that there was coercion exerted directly against him in the belief or practice of his religion. On the other hand, in order to challenge a law as a violation of the second religious clause of the Amendment, the one guarding against a prohibition of the "free exercise" of religion, mere economic injury, no matter how great and no matter how uniquely it affected the would-be litigant, was not enough. To raise a "free exercise" challenge to a law, the challenger had to show that the law, or its application, placed a coercive restriction upon his own religious belief or practice. Thus, to raise a free exercise issue, it was necessary to show coercion, while "standing" to raise an establishment clause issue would be found if there were either coercion or economic injury to the plaintiff. At least this was the law prior to 1962. In the Regents' Prayer case, however, the Court found that the complainants had standing to raise the establishment clause question even though they suffered no measurable economic injury beyond their interest as taxpayers. Nor were they really coerced to perform any act or assent to any prayer, although the Court there and in the 1963 Schempp case indicated that there might be "coercion" from the mere existence of "laws officially prescribing a particular form of worship."[3] In the Schempp case, where the complaining parties suffered no economic injury beyond the expenditure of tax funds, the Court practically read the economic standing requirement out of existence: "The parties here are school children and their parents, who are directly affected by the laws and practices against which their complaints are directed. These interests surely suffice to give the parties standing to complain."[4] Nor was there any real coercion of the complaining children in the Schempp case.

So, without any economic interest of the complainants affected, and even without any actual coercion of their beliefs, the Court recognized their standing to compel a decision. It is difficult to believe that this Court, assuming the continuance of its present tendency, will feel constrained by the doctrine of standing to avoid a decision of any religious liberty question which it cares to decide. This result is unfortunate, for some matters are better left untouched by the Supreme Court and are better entrusted to the good sense of the people locally involved or to the decision of lower courts. In some situations, a rigid rule applying uniformly throughout the nation can be productive of more confusion than guidance. Let us hope, then, that the Supreme Court will once again recognize the utility of the standing rule in religion cases.[5]

RESPECT FOR LOCAL SELF-GOVERNMENT

Apart from the doctrine of standing, there is another salutary rule of interpretation that should be applied by the Supreme Court in religion cases. The Court has now held that the Fourteenth Amendment, when it prohibited the states from depriving any person of life, liberty or property without due process of law, made applicable to the states the restrictions of the First Amendment which had originally restricted only the federal government. In the Schempp case, the Court said that the First Amendment was thus made "wholly applicable to the states," rendering them "as incompetent as Congress" in the area of religion.[6] Yet, in applying the Fifth Amendment to the states through the Fourteenth, the Court has held, for example, that the states are not prohibited to the same extent as Congress from imposing double jeopardy on criminal defendants. Thus one of the great American judges, Mr. Justice Cardozo, wrote the opinion for the Court in the 1937 case of *Palko v. Connecticut*[7] where the Court held that Connecticut could properly re-try and convict a defendant whose first trial contained error which caused his acquittal. Connecticut could do so even though Congress, which is subject to the direct restrictions of the Fifth Amendment, could not. Cardozo said that the Fourteenth Amendment applied to the state only those guarantees of individual rights that are "implicit in the concept of ordered liberty."[8] The Fourteenth Amendment forbids any state to deprive any person of life, liberty or property without due process of law. The meaning of the Cardozo reasoning is that thereby the Fourteenth Amendment prohibits to the states only those practices which are "repugnant to the conscience of mankind."[9] The states, therefore, have greater latitude than Congress in dealing with such matters covered by the Fifth Amendment. The same principle was applied by the Supreme Court to the privilege against self-incrimination, also contained in the Fifth Amendment, as early as 1908.[10] The principle of the Palko case has since been reaffirmed by the Court.[11]

It would be wise for the Supreme Court to apply a similar rule to the First Amendment religion clauses, affording to the states and local governments a greater latitude and flexibility in dealing with religion than Congress enjoys. It is, after all, a federal Constitution, in which the Tenth Amendment provides: "The powers not delegated to the United States by the Constitution, nor prohibited by it to the States, are reserved to the States respectively or to the people." The Tenth Amendment is a part of the Bill of Rights, and it became effective on the same day as the First Amendment. While the Tenth Amendment is a restatement of the obvious —that powers delegated to the federal government are delegated and powers not delegated are retained by the states or the people—it ought to have vitality at least as a guide for determining the extent and character of the powers delegated. The United States Constitution is premised in its division of powers upon the principle of subsidiarity, that governmental functions are best entrusted to the lowest level of government able to accomplish them. To be sure, there are some powers which are denied therein to any government at any level, such as the power to deprive a person of life, liberty or property without "due process of law." But the school prayer decisions raise the question whether the federal government can or should intervene to prevent those citizens who wish to do so from acknowledging God in their public events. It violates the federate character of the Constitution to say that this is a question that cries for a uniform national solution, unless the local practice in question is so gross as to be "repugnant to the conscience of mankind," in Cardozo's phrase. Surely, the inclusion of Bible reading or a prayer, whether the Lord's Prayer or one as nearly non-denominational as possible, into the public school day, with a scrupulous prevention of real coercion of those who choose not to participate, is not so repugnant, in view of the history and tradition of the American people.

It would be better for the Supreme Court to adopt an attitude of healthy respect for the general fairness and ability of local agencies to solve local problems, and a healthy recognition of the limitations inherent in any effort to rule a diversified nation by uniform, centralized decree. Such a misguided effort to carry the responsibilities of a Supreme School Board can only result in a lessening of the diversity upon which we have thrived, or a frustration and stultification of the Court itself. Neither is a good result.

CONSTRUCTION OF THE ESTABLISHMENT CLAUSE

Of course, there are limits to the powers of local governments. In the area of religion, those limits are found principally in the First Amendment. The Supreme Court, then, while requiring that litigants possess a substantial interest, arising from economic loss or coercion, to raise substantial issues, and while deferring reasonably to the prerogatives of the people and their local or state governments, must be ready on an appropriate occasion to apply the sanctions of the First Amendment to state or local action.

In thus applying the establishment clause, which prohibits any "law respecting an establishment of religion," the Court should free itself of its uncritical adherence to what Mr. Justice Stewart aptly called "resounding but fallacious fundamentalist rhetoric."[12] Specifically, the Court ought frankly to discard its conclusion that, in the words of the Everson decision, government is "stripped of all power . . . to support, or otherwise to assist any or all religions. . . ."[13] The Court should realize that there can be no inviolate governmental neutrality between theistic and non-theistic religions, because government cannot deny, or suspend judgment upon, the existence of God without adopting the tenets of atheism or agnosticism. Given our history and the manifest desire of the people, government in the United States not only can, but ought, to affirm the essential truths of the existence of God and His providential concern for human affairs. By that affirmation, government would in fact "aid" theistic religions. But a contrary result, through the adoption of the non-theistic view, would "aid" non-theistic religions, as well as give the lie to the Declaration of Independence. And it should be recognized, of course, that every type of non-preferential financial aid to all religions, theistic and non-theistic, ought not to be rigidly proscribed in advance by an abstract and inflexible construction of the First Amendment.

It is usually asserted that, if we allow the Regents' Prayer, the Lord's Prayer or Bible reading into public events, it will be impossible to prevent those religious elements from becoming more and more sectarian. If we grant the power in the first instance, it is said, what is to prevent a Catholic-dominated school board from including a communal rosary as part of the opening exercises in the public schools? The answer is twofold. The good sense of the community involved can usually be counted on to prevent religious observances from being carried to a sectarian excess. Secondly, if excesses do occur, the courts, including the Supreme Court, can readily deal with them. But the courts should do so, not through the ritualistic invocation of metaphors or formulae, but rather through a determination that, in the particular case, the line has been crossed and the local government has embarked upon an inadmissibly sectarian program. Where should the line be drawn? Clearly, it ought not to be drawn to prohibit the Lord's Prayer, Bible reading or something like the Regents' Prayer. Should a school board dominated, for instance, by Moslems, be able to introduce the voluntary devotional reading of the Koran into a public school in which Moslems are in the majority? Yes. Certainly, however, some outright sectarian rituals ought to be barred. The Mass, for example, should not become part of the public school day, even on a voluntary basis. But the line should be drawn case-by-case, and not through the promulgation in advance of an impractically rigid general rule. Moreover, if past experience is a reliable guide, cases of excess will be few and far between.

In short, then, let us hope that the Court will renounce its adherence to abstract prohibitions which can be effected only at the ultimate cost of the religious freedom they are supposed to protect. And let us hope that the Court will realize that the Constitution and religious liberty alike will best be served in an atmosphere of governmental encouragement of belief in God and hospitality to all religious creeds.

CONSTRUCTION OF THE FREE EXERCISE CLAUSE

The school prayer decisions rested upon the establishment clause of the First Amendment, although in each case the Court indicated that the religious exercise in question might also violate the free exercise clause of the Amendment. It is claimed by some that the inclusion of religious observances in public ceremonies violates the free exercise clause, in that persons who conscientiously object must expose themselves to embarrassment by withdrawing from them. Thereby, it is said, they are denied the full and free exercise of their religion. Since the Court has indicated it approves this contention, any proposal for reorientation of the Court's prayer decisions must include an evaluation of the free exercise clause and its implications.

The free exercise clause is designed to forbid the government "to force the conscience" of men or "to punish them for worshipping God in the manner which they believe their accountability to him requires."[14] Some type of coercion of the individual must exist in order to have a violation of the free exercise clause. The establishment clause, on the other hand, "does not depend upon any showing of direct governmental compulsion and is violated by the enactment of laws which establish an official religion whether those laws operate directly to coerce nonobserving individuals or not."[15] We have examined at pages 45–49 the specific and limited nature of the "establishment" which this clause was designed to prevent.

In terms of the free exercise clause, a frank compulsion of an individual to declare a religious belief or to participate in a public ceremony which includes a declaration of a religious belief, is clearly unconstitutional coercion. Thus, a school child who entertains "religious scruples" against the practice may not be compelled to salute the flag.[16] The existence of a reasonable opportunity to refrain from such a declaration or to withdraw from participation in the offensive ceremony, however, should prevent the Court from finding unconstitutional coercion. Moreover, the fact that his withholding of participation brings some inconvenience or embarrassment to the objector, ought not of itself to prevent the opportunity of refraining or withdrawing from being effective as a safeguard of the free exercise of religion. At least this is so where the inconvenience or embarrassment is not unreasonably great. In the flag salute case, *Board of Education v. Barnette,* in 1943, it was not embarrassment but the total absence of an opportunity for withdrawal which made it unconstitutional to compel the objecting child to salute the flag. In *Hamilton v. Regents,*[17] decided in 1934, the State of California compelled students at the State University to take a military training course as a condition of attendance at the school. The Supreme Court agreed without dissent that there was no violation of an objecting student's free exercise of religion. The student had an opportunity to withdraw from the situation which offended his religious scruples. This opportunity was reasonable even though the student could avail himself of it only at the cost of abandoning his chance for an education at a state-supported school.

It is, of course, difficult to define with finality at what point the inconvenience involved in his withholding of participation becomes too great, and therefore the objector's free exercise of religion is infringed despite his option not to participate. When the Court considered in 1961 the provision of the Maryland constitution requiring state employees to declare their belief in God, it held that the loss of an opportunity for state employment is an unreasonable imposition upon the objecting applicant's "freedom of belief and religion."[18] Perhaps, in view of this holding, the Court would decide the Hamilton case differently if it were presented today. Even so, both cases involved burdens upon the individual which were clearly greater than that involved in subjecting a nonbeliever to the embarrassment of keeping silent during a public prayer or temporarily leaving the room. Obviously, the pressures upon the California student to take the military training or forfeit his opportunity for an education at his state university, and upon the Maryland applicant for state employment to declare his belief in God or forfeit the job, were greater than those upon the student who chooses not to participate in a non-compulsory prayer. It is fair to say that those who find a fatal coercion in the usual school prayer situation will have to look elsewhere than to the pre-1962 opinions of the Supreme Court for precedent to support their conclusion. The current majority of the Court, who evidently believe that there is coercion there, appear to have looked no further than their own preconceptions.[19]

Unless the Court is determined to say that no public prayer situation can avoid a violation of the free exercise clause, and no amount of solicitude for the sensibilities of objectors can cure the presumed defect, then the Court should resurrect the rule of the Barnette case of 1943. There the Court properly ruled that the Jehovah's Witness could not be compelled to participate in the flag salute to which he had religious objections. But the Court did not say that everyone else had to forego the salute. So also in the public prayer situation. None will deny that all practicable precautions must be taken to shield the objector from open or covert coercion. But he ought not to be given the power, at his whim, to stop a public avowal of faith which the majority wishes to perform and which is in harmony with our national tradition. The current Supreme Court, unfortunately, has shown an extravagant regard for the imagined sensibilities of a vociferous minority. Building upon its own casual remarks in prior cases, the Court has not only unjustly disadvantaged the majority, but in so doing has relegated an important strain of our national tradition to the museum of antiquity.

Moreover, the Court has lost sight of the right of the majority of citizens to the free exercise of their religion. The opinion of the Court in the Schempp case denied that the decision infringed the majority's right to free exercise of religion. The free exercise clause, said the Court, "has never meant that a majority could use the machinery of the State to practice its religion."[20] But that reasoning collides with the fact that the prayer decisions permit a minority to use the machinery of the state to affirm the basic truth of its non-theistic religion, while the theistic majority is precluded from so doing. It would better promote the free exercise of religion by all if the Court would step out of the way, avoid intervention, and permit the citizens of the localities involved to express their belief or non-belief in God as they see fit. Intervention by the courts, acting under the free exercise clause, should come only to prevent actual coercion of beliefs or non-beliefs.

The Court may soon have an opportunity to define its position in this "free exercise" area. After the 1963 Supreme Court decision in the Schempp case, the New York State Department of Education issued instructions that ruled out all vocal prayer in the public school classrooms of that state and left room only for a period of silent meditation. In line with this policy, the principal of Public School 184 in Whitestone ordered the kindergarten children to cease reciting a morning prayer and singing an afternoon religious song. The morning prayer was:

God is great, God is good
And we thank Him for our food, Amen.

The afternoon classes sang:

Thank You for the World So Sweet
Thank You for the food we eat
Thank You for the birds that sing
Thank You, God for everything.

The pupils were led in the prayer and song by the teacher, or the teacher merely stood permissively by without participating. There was no state law or regulation requiring or permitting the practice. When the principal, acting upon the protest of a parent, stopped the practice, the parents of 15 of the 200 kindergarten children organized a group which they called PRAY (Prayer Rights for American Youth), retained a local attorney, and sued in the federal court in Brooklyn to enjoin the school authorities from interfering with the practice. On December 20, 1963, District Judge Walter Bruchhausen, in the case of *Stein v. Oshinsky,* upheld the parents and enjoined the school authorities from interfering with the prayers. Judge Bruchhausen wrote:

> The case . . . does not involve a state statute requiring the children or personnel to engage actively in or refrain from acknowledging their complete dependence upon God. It is merely a voluntary desire of the children without coercion or pressure being brought to offer a prayer to the Almighty.[21]

It is likely that this case, or some other one posing the same issue, will find its way to the Supreme Court. When it does, the learned Justices will have to decide whether these children, who persist in wanting to thank God as well as the state for their cookies and milk, pose too grave a threat to the Republic to be endured. Unfortunately, this Court may conclude that if the teacher stands idly and permissively by while the children pray, or even more so if the teacher joins in or leads the prayer, the prayers take on an official color and the teacher is thereby "sanctioning official prayers," contrary to Justice Black's dictum in *Engel v. Vitale* that "each separate government in this country should stay out of the business of writing or sanctioning official prayers. . . ."[22] And if the Court does forbid these toddlers to pray when they want to, the decision predictably will be hailed as a proper rebuff to "divisiveness." And then, having written into the judge-made law the precept that citizens cannot pray on public property, even voluntarily, the sanctimonious enemies of discord will resume their strident—and truly divisive—attacks upon the remaining vestiges of the public tradition that this is a nation subordinate to God.

Obviously, the establishment and free exercise clauses are related. Properly construed, the establishment clause is ancillary, since, as Mr. Justice Stewart has emphasized in the Schempp case, "the central value embodied in the First Amendment . . . is the safeguarding of an individual's right to free exercise of his religion. . . ."[23] If we dare to hope for an eventual reorientation of its views by the Court, let us realize that it can be done well only through a coherent and sensible construction of both clauses of the Amendment and their interaction.

IX

1. *Frothingham v. Mellon,* 262 U.S. 447 (1923).
2. 262 U.S. at 486–87.
3. *Engel v. Vitale,* 370 U.S. 421, 431 (1962); *Abington Township v. Schempp,* 374 U.S. 203, 221 (1963).
4. 374 U.S. at 224.
5. For a discussion of the "standing" issues in religion cases, see *McGowan v. Maryland,* 366 U.S. 420, 429–430 (1961).
6. 374 U.S. at 215.
7. 302 U.S. 319 (1937).
8. 302 U.S. at 325.
9. 302 U.S. at 323.
10. *Twining v. New Jersey,* 211 U.S. 78 (1908).
11. *Brock v. North Carolina,* 344 U.S. 424 (1953).
12. *Sherbert v. Verner,* 374 U.S. 398, 416 (1963).
13. 330 U.S. at 11.
14. Story, *Commentaries on the Constitution of the United States* (Boston, 1891), sec. 1876.
15. *Engel v. Vitale,* 370 U.S. 421, 430 (1962).
16. *Board of Education v. Barnette,* 319 U.S. 624 (1943).
17. 293 U.S. 245 (1934).
18. *Torcaso v. Watkins,* 367 U.S. 488 (1961).
19. See *Engel v. Vitale,* 370 U.S. 421, 430–31 (1962); *Abington Township v. Schempp,* 374 U.S. 203, 221 (1963).

20. 374 U.S. at 226.
21. *Stein v. Oshinsky,* 224 F. Supp. 757 (E.D.N.Y., 1963); *New York Times,* December 21, 1963.
22. 370 U.S. at 435.
23. 374 U.S. at 312.

I believe the decision was improperly made and I go for reversing it.

ABRAHAM LINCOLN
on The Dred Scott Decision

X

Solution by Legislation or Constitutional Amendment

Unfortunately, this Supreme Court is not likely to reverse itself on the issue of public prayer. Congress, however, can limit the appellate jurisdiction of the Court, or propose a constitutional amendment for ratification by the states.

The Constitution, in defining the powers of the Supreme Court, provides:

> In all Cases affecting ambassadors, other public ministers and consuls, and those in which a state shall be party, the supreme court shall have original jurisdiction. In all the other cases . . . , the supreme court shall have appellate jurisdiction, both as to law and fact, *with such exceptions, and under such regulations as the Congress shall make*[1] (Italics added).

Congress, therefore, can prohibit the Court from hearing appeals in any or all cases. A simple Act of Congress, requiring a majority vote, or two-thirds in the event of a presidential veto, would be sufficient for this purpose. In one celebrated case, *Ex parte McCardle,* in 1869,[2] Congress withdrew the appellate jurisdiction of the Court over a Reconstruction Act case after the Court had already heard the arguments of counsel and while the Court was formulating its decision. Obeying the Congressional mandate, the Court promptly dismissed the appeal. No similar case has occurred since. Nevertheless, the McCardle case is a sound precedent and appears to harmonize with the purpose of the section of Article III which we have just quoted. Properly conceived, the Congressional control over the appellate jurisdiction of the Supreme Court can operate as a salutary feature of the system of "checks and balances"—a system purposely designed to ensure that the legislative, executive and judicial branches of the federal government remain mutually dependent one upon the other, and that therefore no one branch, or two acting together, can control the government. Presumably, the Supreme Court today would follow the McCardle precedent in the event of a withdrawal by Congress of part of its appellate jurisdiction. However, given the inclination of this Court to re-examine precedents in many fields, and the consequent unpredictability of its decisions, submission by the Court to Congress in this regard cannot be foretold with certainty. Needless to say, a refusal by the Court to accede to a limitation by Congress of its appellate jurisdiction would precipitate a genuine constitutional crisis.

If Congress withdrew the Court's appellate jurisdiction over cases involving governmental sponsorship of prayer, the withdrawal would prevent further misinterpretation by the Court. But it would also leave standing the erroneous decisions already rendered, and lower courts would probably consider themselves bound by them, or at least regard them as persuasive, in deciding similar cases. Furthermore, although the Supreme Court's role in religion cases ought to be limited, as we have discussed in Chapter IX, access to the Court should not be totally foreclosed in advance. There may be some cases, such as those involving actual coercion of dissidents, in which adjudication by the highest court would resolve glaring inconsistencies in lower court decisions or correct an obvious miscarriage of justice. The abstractionist members now on the Court have done damage enough by their simplistic interpretations. We should be reluctant to permit the error of their ways to compel a partial abolition of the Supreme Court itself as an effective agency of government.

For these reasons, a withdrawal of the Court's jurisdiction would not be the most desirable solution. On the whole, a constitutional amendment would provide a better remedy.

But it is one thing to talk about an amendment and another to draft one. It is extremely difficult to draft any law that cannot be misconstrued by the courts. This ever-present possibility of misinterpretation assumes commanding importance in the drafting of an amendment which would ultimately go for interpretation to the same Supreme Court which occasioned the amendment by its misconstructions in the first place. A new amendment, moreover, ideally should be broad enough to cover all those government-sponsored religious observances which have been drawn into question by the school prayer decisions to date. A constitutional amendment can be adopted in two ways. It can be initiated by a two-thirds majority in the House of Representatives and Senate, in which case it must then be approved by three-fourths of the state legislatures, or by conventions in three-fourths of the states, if Congress prescribes that ratification shall be by conventions rather than by the state legislatures. Only one amendment has been so adopted by state conventions—the Twenty-first Amendment, which repealed Prohibition in 1933. All the rest have been approved by state legislatures. The second method of amending the Constitution is that, "on the application of the Legislatures of two-thirds of the several States," the Congress "shall call a Convention for proposing Amendments," which shall be valid upon ratification thereafter by the legislatures or conventions, as Congress may prescribe, in three-quarters of the states.[3] The President cannot veto a constitutional amendment and his approval is not required. The amending process is a matter for the Congress and the states.

Dozens of amendments, of various types, have been proposed in Congress to reverse the school prayer decisions. On July 26 and August 2, 1962, hearings on several such proposals were conducted by the Senate Committee on the Judiciary. But no further action has been taken by the Senate to approve any of the amendments. The failure of the Senate to move is explainable largely by the fact that, in the House of Representatives, the Committee on the Judiciary, chaired by Representative Emanuel Celler, a Democrat from Brooklyn, New York, has been slow to act on the subject. It is desirable that there be close and continued cooperation between the House and Senate in processing a constitutional amendment, which depends for its approval upon a two-thirds majority in each chamber. It would be futile for the Senate to deliberate the matter fully if there were no hope of comparable action in the House of Representatives. Therefore, in practical terms, the cause of a public prayer amendment is frustrated by the inaction of the House Judiciary Committee.

The House of Representatives, like the Senate, operates very much according to settled procedures. One such procedure is the generally useful one that no resolution or bill shall be considered by the House as a whole until the relevant committee has held hearings on it and reported its recommendations. One way, however, in which a committee can be bypassed, and a resolution or bill can be considered by the House without prior hearings and report, is for a majority of the members (218 of 435) to sign a discharge petition. Thereupon, the resolution or bill will be brought, without further hearings or committee report, directly to the floor of the House for debate, amendment if desired, and a vote. When it became apparent that the Judiciary Committee was acting too slowly on the more than one hundred resolutions proposing prayer amendments, Congressman Frank J. Becker, Republican of Lynbrook, New York, filed Discharge Petition No. 3 on July 9, 1963. The petition, if signed by 218 House members, would bring to the floor an amendment resolution, House Joint Resolution 693,[4] which was drafted by an ad hoc committee of six Congressmen (Representatives Becker, who was chairman; Walter S. Baring, Democrat of Nevada; William C. Cramer, Republican of Florida; Horace R. Kornegay, Democrat of North Carolina; Delbert L. Latta, Republican of Ohio; Don Fuqua, Democrat of Florida) who had been named at a meeting of about fifty interested members of the House. The entire text of H. J. Res. 693 provides:

JOINT RESOLUTION

Proposing an amendment to the Constitution of the United States

Resolved by the Senate and House of Representatives of the United States of America in Congress assembled (two-thirds of each House concurring therein), That the following article is hereby proposed as an amendment to the Constitution of the United States, which shall be valid to all intents and purposes as part of the Constitution only if ratified by the legislatures of three-fourths of the several States within seven years from the date of its submission to the States by the Congress:

ARTICLE—

SEC. 1. Nothing in this Constitution shall be deemed to prohibit the offering, reading from, or listening to prayers or biblical scriptures, if participation therein is on a voluntary basis, in any governmental or public school, institution, or place.

SEC. 2. Nothing in this Constitution shall be deemed to prohibit making reference to belief in, reliance upon, or invoking the aid of God or a Supreme Being in any governmental or public document, proceeding, activity, ceremony, school, institution, or place, or upon any coinage, currency, or obligation of the United States.

SEC. 3. Nothing in this article shall constitute an establishment of religion.

SEC. 4. This article shall be inoperative unless it shall have been ratified as an amendment to the Constitution by the legislatures of three-fourths of the several States within seven years from the date of its submission to the States by the Congress.

As of March 13, 1964, only 161 Congressmen had signed the petition, which remains in effect until the end of the 88th Congress sometime in 1964. The disparity between the large number of House members who appear to favor a prayer amendment, and the lesser number who have signed the petition, is due to an ingrained, and understandable, Congressional reluctance to bypass committees. In view of that strong reluctance, the progress made by the petition is encouraging. It is highly doubtful that enough signatures can be obtained before adjournment of the 88th Congress. If so, and if the Judiciary Committee continues its reluctance to act, a successor petition will undoubtedly be filed in the 89th Congress, which will convene in January, 1965.

On its merits, H. J. Res. 693 is worthy of support as a catalyst to bring the subject to the floor of the House. Its sponsors do not claim perfection for it, and in several respects it does require clarification. It may be helpful here to discuss a few ways in which it might be improved when it is resubmitted in the next session of Congress, or when and if it finally does come to the floor of the House for debate, amendment and vote. For example, in Section 1, the prayer or scripture reading is not prohibited "if participation therein is on a voluntary basis." In the school prayer cases to date, no one was compelled to join in the prayer or scripture reading. Even so, in addition to its actual holding that the procedures constituted a "law respecting an establishment of religion," and therefore violated the establishment clause of the First Amendment, the Supreme Court majority, in both the Engel and Schempp decisions, indicated its belief that the procedures were inherently coercive and therefore violative of the free exercise clause of the First Amendment. Presumably, the Court meant there that when students suffer embarrassment as the price of their non-participation, then their participation is coerced and not "on a voluntary basis." H. J. Res. 693 would not clearly bar the Court from ruling that the amendment was designed to validate only those prayer procedures where participation is "voluntary" under present judicial standards. That is, the Court could say the amendment was not designed to validate the school prayer procedures used in the Engel and Schempp cases, in which procedures the participation is not truly "voluntary." At least, there is nothing in the word "voluntary" of Section 1 to prevent such a misinterpretation by the Court. It would be more definitive for the amendment to spell out an understanding that the type of coercion that will make participation in the exercise involuntary is a coercion greater than the sort of embarrassment inflicted upon non-participants in the Engel and Schempp situations. Perhaps it would be helpful for the amendment to read here, "if actual participation therein is not compulsory."

The phrasing of Section 2, "prohibit making reference to belief in, reliance upon, or invoking the aid of God . . .," is gramatically confusing. Perhaps it would be clearer if it read, "prohibit making reference to belief in or reliance upon, or invoking the aid of, God or a Supreme Being. . . ."

Section 3 in its entirety appears to be superfluous. The only arguable justification for it would appear to be a fear that the Supreme Court would construe the amendment as not modifying the establishment clause. In other words, the Court would say that, regardless of the prayer amendment, the establishment clause of the First Amendment is so preeminent that no amendment can be deemed to restrict it unless that restricting amendment expressly says so. This is really reasoning in a circle. The opening phrase of H. J. Res. 693, "Nothing in this Constitution shall be deemed to prohibit," is about as encompassing a negation as can be drafted. It would seem to indicate clearly, unless it were specifically provided otherwise in the amendment, that the establishment clause shall no longer operate to invalidate any of the mentioned practices. If we are to engraft the wording of Section 3 upon an amendment, then perhaps we ought also to specify that nothing in the amendment shall constitute a prohibition of the free exercise of religion, and nothing in the amendment shall constitute a religious test oath, or an infringement of freedom of association, or of freedom of speech, etc.

A more serious defect in H. J. Res. 693, is its failure to cover the problem of governmental financial aid to religion. The sponsors of the amendment are hopeful that the present language will safeguard the chaplaincies in the armed forces, legislatures and prisons. Unfortunately, the main objection raised to chaplaincies is not merely that chaplains conduct religious services as a part of governmental activities (an objection which appears to be obliquely but satisfactorily met in Section 2), but more importantly that chaplains are financed by government. The language of Section 2 could be construed to permit chaplains to function in the armed forces and elsewhere, that is, with government facilities, but at the same time to strike them from the public payroll. It is important to close this loophole, since the Supreme Court in the Schempp case indicated that it may view with favor the distinction between privately-paid chaplains using "government facilities" and chaplains on the public payroll.[5] Chaplaincies, at public expense, ought to be specifically mentioned in the amendment. H. J. Res. 693 is defective also in that it does not specifically approve the tax privileges which are now generally accorded to religious bodies. This form of governmental financing of religion is under sustained attack, it is now in litigation, and it will probably be decided by the Supreme Court in the next few years. The tax privileges also ought to be specifically protected.

In the nature of the political process, an expansion of the amendment to cover government financial aid to religion could jeopardize its passage. Some who oppose the prayer decisions sincerely doubt the constitutionality of general federal aid to religious schools. Presumably, the support which some would give to an amendment restricted to the prayer aspect, would be withdrawn from an amendment which attempted to validate federal aid to parochial schools. Several factors must be considered here. So far, the Supreme Court's aberrations in the school prayer cases have not developed into a judicial crusade against federal aid to parochial schools. On the contrary, it is likely that some forms of tax credits or tax deductions to offset the cost of parochial education, and perhaps restricted federal grants or loans to religious schools or their pupils, would be upheld even by the Court today.[6] This is especially so in the light of *Sherbert v. Verner,* the South Carolina unemployment compensation case, which was decided on the same day in 1963 as the Schempp case and which reaffirmed that religious adherents may not be excluded, because of their faith or lack of it, from the benefits of public welfare legislation.[7] In short, the danger to federal aid to church schools is not as great or immediate as the peril to the tax privileges of religious groups.[8] While it would be neater for a prayer amendment to cover the ancillary question of aid to education, it may not be possible to do so, given the practical order of things. We must define, therefore, a hierarchy of needs, and the restoration of public prayer, the safeguarding of tax privileges, and the protection of chaplaincies, should rank higher in the scale than the difficult, and maybe unnecessary, specification of the constitutional status of aid to parochial schools. Although tax privileges and chaplaincies themselves involve governmental financial support of religion, they seem to have precipitated far less of a division among those who would support a public prayer amendment than has the aid to education question. The inclusion of a specific validation of tax privileges and chaplaincies would therefore not jeopardize the passage of an amendment nearly as much as would the inclusion of an aid to education provision. Also relevant is the fact that tax privileges are far more essential to the preservation of religion than is federal aid to parochial schools. It would be a mistake, therefore, for those, including this writer, who are convinced of the constitutionality of some forms of federal aid to church-related schools, to condition their support of a prayer amendment upon its validation of such aid.

As a final observation on the text of H. J. Res. 693, a cautionary clause would seem to be in order, to emphasize that the amendment is not to be construed to imply that any unmentioned practices or religious observances are unconstitutional because they are not specifically mentioned in the amendment. Such a clause might read, "Nothing in this amendment shall be construed to imply that any practice, program or activity is unconsitutional because it is not mentioned herein." This device would forestall the application to the amendment of the legal maxim, "expressio unius est exclusio alterius"—the expression of one thing implies the exclusion of others. Although the negative phrasing of the amendment, "Nothing in this Constitution shall be deemed to prohibit," would normally prevent the operation of the exclusionary maxim, and although the language of Sections 1 and 2 is quite sweeping in its reach, it would be better to remove all doubt on this score. Such a cautionary clause, for example, would prevent the application of the exclusionary maxim to federal aid to parochial schools or to any other practice, program or activity not mentioned in the amendment.

This extended discussion of H. J. Res. 693 is not intended to detract from other prayer amendments which have been proposed in the Senate and House, or which may be proposed in future sessions of the Congress. Senators Barry Goldwater of Arizona, A. Willis Robertson of Virginia, John Stennis of Mississippi and Strom Thurmond of South Carolina have been particularly active in working for an amendment, and numerous other Senators and Representatives have been similarly outspoken and effective. Our concentration here on H. J. Res. 693 springs from two main considerations. First, the language does represent a consensus of an ad hoc committee of more than 50 Representatives, and while it cannot be inferred that each of them, or even each member of the six-man subcommittee which drafted it, agrees fully with the wording of the amendment, nevertheless the language is notable as the product of sustained and intensive consideration by a substantial and competent group of legislators. Secondly, because of the obstruction in the House Committee on the Judiciary, H. J. Res. 693 has become the focus of the amendment drive at this time.

Unanimity on the phrasing of an amendment will be impossible of full achievement. Yet all those who seek to rectify the absurdities and ills of the Supreme Court's First Amendment posturings, are well advised to support the drive for a constitutional amendment. Congressman Becker, the sponsor of the pending discharge petition, has noted that the main obstacle to its success is public apathy. Many Congressmen have not signed the discharge petition because their constituents have not shown them that they support it. Public opinion polls have continually demonstrated that the American public disagrees with the school prayer decisions. Yet, in too many quarters, the long-term reaction to the rulings has been one of passive acquiescence. It is an acquiescence undoubtedly born in large part of a deep-rooted respect for law and for the Supreme Court as the highest judicial organ of law. Ironically, though, respect for the Court is misdirected insofar as it engenders a docile submission to decisions which, in a real sense, can themselves be described as lawless. We should respect the Supreme Court as an institution. But it is in the long-term interest of the Court, and the nation, that this respect should not become a servile abasement.

There are encouraging signs that the latent dissatisfaction of the people is becoming more coherent and organized. Numerous organizations have been formed on the local level, and some on a national scale, to marshal public opinion and to forestall extreme local implementations of the decisions.[9] Let us hope that the drive for an appropriate prayer amendment is just beginning. Surely, this is a cause that merits the support of all Americans who are convinced that this nation is indeed under God, that the Constitution is not simply what a majority of the Supreme Court says it is, and that the national welfare demands an unstinting effort, by government and citizens alike, to rebuild the moral foundations of our strength. It is a cause which transcends denominational differences, and it is one of surpassing importance.

There are some opponents of the school prayer decisions who counsel against amending the Constitution and advance the hope that some day the Supreme Court will respond to argument and brings its decisions back into line with the Constitution and the temper of the people. Perhaps they are right. But the Justices of the Supreme Court majority have shown an uncritical adherence to their own abstractions. It would be less than prudent to rely upon their capacity to admit and correct their own mistakes. In 1857, the United States Supreme Court held, in the notorious Dred Scott case,[10] that a Negro could not be a citizen of the United States. Abraham Lincoln, in his last debate with Senator Stephen Douglas, at Alton, Illinois, on October 15, 1858, said of that decision, "I believe the decision was improperly made and I go for reversing it."[11] We can, with equal right, pass the same judgment upon the school prayer decisions. Let us go for reversing them. The Constitution provides a remedy through the process of amendment—in this case an amendment, not to change the Constitution, but to restore it. In a matter so vital, that remedy ought to be employed without delay.

X

1. Art. III, Section 2, clause 2.
2. 7 Wallace (U.S.) 506 (1869).
3. United States Constitution, Article V.
4. H. J. Res. 693 (88th Cong., 1st Sess.).
5. 374 U.S. at 226.
6. See above, p. 89.
7. See above, p. 91.
8. Tax privileges are discussed above in Chapter VI. Chaplains are treated on pp. 21, 111.
9. Two such national groups are: Citizens for Public Prayer, Box 1776, Rutland, Massachusetts, and Constitutional Prayer Foundation, 901 Munsey Building, Baltimore, Maryland.
10. *Scott v. Sandford,* 19 Howard (U.S.) 393 (1857).
11. *The Works of Abraham Lincoln,* Federal Edition (1905), IV, 215 ff.

APPENDIX A

Recognition of God in Colonial Public Documents*

MAGNA CARTA, June 12, 1215

John, by the grace of God, king of England, Lord of Ireland, duke of Normandy and Aquitaine, count of Anjou, to the archbishops, bishops, abbots, earls, barons, justiciars, foresters, sheriffs, reeves, servants, and all bailiffs and his faithful people greeting. Know that by the inspiration of God and for the good of our soul and those of all our predecessors and of our heirs, to the honor of God and the exaltation of holy church, and the improvement of our kingdom, by the advice of our venerable fathers. . . .

FIRST CHARTER OF VIRGINIA, April 10, 1606

We, greatly commending, and graciously accepting of, their Desires for the Furtherance of so noble a Work, which may, by the Providence of Almighty God, hereafter tend to the Glory of his Divine Majesty, in propagating of *Christian* Religion to such People, as yet live in Darkness and miserable Ignorance of the true Knowledge and Worship of God, and may in time bring the Infidels and Savages, living in those parts, to human Civility, and to a settled and quiet Government; DO, by these our Letters Patents, graciously accept of, and agree to, their humble and well-intended Desires.

* *Sources of Our Liberties,* Perry, ed. (New York, 1952). See p. 27 above.

ORDINANCES FOR VIRGINIA, July 24, 1621

KNOW YE, that we, the said Treasurer, Council, and Company, taking into our careful Consideration the present State of the said Colony of *Virginia,* and intending, by the Divine Assistance, to settle such a Form of Government there, as may be to the greatest Benefit and Comfort of the People. . . .

MAYFLOWER COMPACT, November 11, 1620

IN THE NAME OF GOD, AMEN. We, whose names are underwritten, the Loyal Subjects of our dread Sovereign Lord King *James,* by the grace of God, of *Great Britain, France,* and *Ireland,* King, *Defender of the Faith,* &c. Having undertaken for the Glory of God, and Advancement of the Christian Faith, and the Honour of our King and Country, a Voyage to plant the first Colony in the northern Parts of *Virginia;* Do by these Presents, solemnly and mutually, in the Presence of God and one another, covenant and combine ourselves together into a civil Body Politick, for our better Ordering and Preservation, and Furtherance of the Ends aforesaid. . . .

CHARTER OF MASSACHUSETTS BAY, March 4, 1629

CHARLES, BY THE GRACE OF GOD, Kinge of England, Scotland, Fraunce, and Ireland, Defendor of the Fayth, &c. TO ALL to whome theis Presents shall come Greeting. . . .

. . . whereby our said People, Inhabitants there, may be soe religiously, peaceablie, and civilly governed, as their good Life and orderlie Conversacon, maie wynn and incite the Natives of Country, to the Knowledge and Obedience of the onlie true God and Sauior of Mankinde, and the Christian Fayth, which in our Royall Intencon, and the Adventurers free Profession, is the principall Ende of this Plantacion.

CHARTER OF MARYLAND, June 20, 1632

Charles, by the Grace of God, of England, Scotland, France, and Ireland, king, Defender of the Faith, &c. To all to whom these Presents come, Greeting.

II. Whereas our well beloved and right trusty Subject Caecilius Calvert, Baron of Baltimore, in our Kingdom of Ireland, Son and Heir of George Calvert, Knight, late Baron of steps of his Father, being animated with a laudable, and Baltimore, in our said Kingdom of Ireland, treading in the pious Zeal for extending the Christian Religion, and also the Territories of our Empire, hath humbly besought Leave of us, that he may transport, by his own Industry, and Expense, a numerous Colony of the English Nation, to a certain Region, herein after described, in a Country hitherto uncultivated, in the Parts of America, and partly occupied by Savages, having no knowledge of the Divine Being, and that all that Region, with some certain Privileges, and Jurisdiction, appertaining unto the wholesome Government, and State of his Colony and Region aforesaid, may by our Royal Highness be given, granted and confirmed unto him, and his Heirs.

FUNDAMENTAL ORDERS OF CONNECTICUT, January 14, 1639

FORASMUCH as it hath pleased the Allmighty God by the wise disposition of his diuyne pruidence so to Order and dispose of things that we the Inhabitants and Residents of Windsor, Harteford and Wethersfield are now cohabiting and dwelling in and vppon the river of Conectecotte and the Lands thereunto adioyneing; And well knowing where a people are gathered togather the word of God requires that to mayntayne the peace and vnion of such a people there should be an orderly and decent Gouerment established according to God, to order and dispose of the affayres of the people at all seasons as occation shall require; doe therefore assotiate and conioyne our selues to be as one Publike State or Com̃onwelth; and doe, for our selues and our Successors and such as shall be adioyned to vs att any tyme hereafter, enter into Combination and Confederation togather, to mayntayne and prsearue the liberty and purity of the gospell of our Lord Jesus wch we now prfesse, as also the disciplyne of the Churches, wch according to the truth of the said gospell is now practised amongst vs; As also in our Ciuell Affaires to be guided and gouerned according to such Lawes, Rules, Orders and decrees as shall be made, ordered & decreed, as followeth. . . .

MASSACHUSETTS BODY OF LIBERTIES, December 10, 1641

A COPPIE OF THE LIBERTIES OF THE MASSACHUSETS COLONIE IN NEW ENGLAND.

The free fruition of such liberties Immunities and priveledges as humanitie, Civilitie, and Christianitie call for as due to every man in his place and proportion without impeachment and Infringement hath ever bene and ever will be the tranquillitie and Stabilitie of Churches and Commonwealths. And the deniall or deprivall thereof, the disturbance if not the ruine of both.

58. Civill Authoritie hath power and libertie to see the peace, ordinances and Rules of Christ observed in every church according to his word. so it be done in a Civill and not in an Ecclesiastical way.
59. Civill Authoritie hath power and libertie to deale with any Church member in a way of Civill Justice, notwithstanding any Church relation, office or interest.
60. No church censure shall degrad or despose any man from any Civill dignitie, office, or Authoritie he shall have in the Commonwealth.

94.

1. If any man after legall conviction shall have or worship any other god, but the lord god, he shall be put to death.
2. If any man or woeman be a witch, (that is hath or consulteth with a familiar spirit,) They shall be put to death.
3. If any man shall Blaspheme the name of god, the father, Sonne or Holie ghost, with direct, expresse, presumptuous or high handed blasphemie, or shall curse god in the like manner, he shall be put to death.

95.

1. All the people of god within this Jurisdiction who are not in a church way, and be orthodox in Judgement, and not scandalous in life, shall have full libertie to gather themselves into a Church Estaite. Provided they doe it in a Christian way, with due observation of the rules of Christ revealed in his word.

10. Wee allowe private meetings for edification in religion amongst Christians of all sortes of people. So it be without just offence for number, time, place, and other cercumstances.

CHARTER OF RHODE ISLAND AND PROVIDENCE PLANTATIONS, July 8, 1663

CHARLES THE SECOND, by the Grace of *God,* King of England, Scotland, France and Ireland, Defender of the Faith, & c., to all to whome these presents shall come, greeting: *Whereas wee* have been informed, by . . . the purchasers and ffree inhabitants of our island, called *Rhode-Island* . . . that they, pursueing, with peaceable and loyall mindes, their sober, serious and religious intentions, of godlie edifieing themselves, and one another, in the holie Christian ffaith and worshipp as they were perswaded; together with the gaineing over and conversione of the poore ignorant Indian natives, in those partes of America, to the sincere professione and obedienc of the same ffaith and worship, did . . . transport themselves out of this kingdome of England into America, . . . where, by the good Providence of God, from whome the Plantationes have taken their name, upon theire labour and industrie, they have not onlie byn preserved to admiration, but have increased and prospered. . . .

FRAME OF GOVERNMENT OF PENNSYLVANIA, April 25, 1682

When the great and wise *God* had made the world, of all his creatures, it pleased him to chuse man his Deputy to rule it: and to fit him for so great a charge and trust, he did not only qualify him with skill and power, but with integrity to use them justly. . . .

This the apostle teaches in divers of his epistles: . . . . "Let every soul be subject to the higher powers; for there is no power but of *God.* The powers that be are ordained of *God:* whosoever therefore resisteth the power, resisteth the ordinance of *God.* For rulers are not a terror to good works, but to evil: wilt thou then not be afraid of the power? do that which is good, and thou shalt have praise of the same." "He is the minister of God to thee for good." "Wherefore ye must needs be subject, not only for wrath, but for conscience sake."

This settles the divine right of government beyond exception, and that for two ends: first, to terrify evil doers: secondly, to cherish those that do well; which gives government a life beyond corruption, and makes it as durable in the world, as good men shall be. So that government seems to me a part of religion itself, a thing sacred in its institution and end. For, if it does not directly remove the cause, it crushes the effects of evil, and is as such, (though a lower, yet) an emanation of the same Divine Power, that is both author and object of pure religion. . . .

PENNSYLVANIA CHARTER OF PRIVILEGES, October 28, 1701

BECAUSE no People can be truly happy, though under the greatest Enjoyment of Civil Liberties, if abridged of the Freedom of their Consciences, as to their Religious Profession and Worship: And Almighty God being the only Lord of Conscience, Father of Lights and Spirits; and the Author as well as Object of all divine Knowledge, Faith and Worship, who only doth enlighten the Minds, and persuade and convince the Understandings of People, I do hereby grant and declare, That no Person or Persons, inhabiting in this Province or Territories, who shall confess and acknowledge *One* almighty God, the Creator, Upholder and Ruler of the World; and profess him or themselves obliged to live quietly under the Civil Government, shall be in any Case molested or prejudiced, in his or their Person or Estate, because of his or their conscientious Persuasion or Practice, nor be compelled to frequent or maintain any religious Worship, Place or Ministry, contrary to his or their Mind, or to do or suffer any other Act or Thing, contrary to their religious Persuasion.

AND that all Persons who also profess to believe in *Jesus Christ,* the Saviour of the World, shall be capable (notwithstanding their other Persuasions and Practices in Point of Conscience and Religion) to serve this Government in any Capacity, both legislatively and executively, he or they solemnly promising, when lawfully required, Allegiance to the King as Sovereign, and Fidelity to the Proprietary and Governor, and taking the Attests as now established by the Law made at *New Castle,* in the Year *One Thousand and Seven Hundred,* entitled, *An Act directing the Attests of several Officers and Ministers,* as now amended and confirmed this present Assembly.

DECLARATION OF THE CAUSES AND NECESSITY OF TAKING UP ARMS, July 6, 1775

But a reverence for our great Creator, principles of humanity, and the dictates of common sense, must convince all those who reflect upon the subject, that government was instituted to promote the welfare of mankind, and ought to be administered for the attainment of that end.

Our cause is just. Our union is perfect. Our internal resources are great, and, if necessary, foreign assistance is undoubtedly attainable.—We gratefully acknowledge, as signal instances of the Divine favour towards us, that his Providence would not permit us to be called into this severe controversy, until we were grown up to our present strength, had been previously exercised in warlike operation, and possessed of the means of defending ourselves. With hearts fortified with these animating reflections, we most solemnly, before God and the world, *declare,* that, exerting the utmost energy of those powers, which our beneficent Creator hath graciously bestowed upon us, the arms we have been compelled by our enemies to assume, we will, in defiance of every hazard, with unabating firmness and perseverence, employ for the preservation of our liberties; being with one mind resolved to die freemen rather than to live slaves.

With an humble confidence in the mercies of the supreme and impartial Judge and Ruler of the Universe, we most devoutly implore his divine goodness to protect us happily through this great conflict, to dispose our adversaries to reconciliation on reasonable terms, and thereby to relieve the empire from the calamities of civil war.

APPENDIX B

Recognition of God in State Constitutions*

ALABAMA

We, the people of the State of Alabama, in order to establish justice, ***, invoking the favor and guidance of Almighty God, do ordain and establish *** (preamble).

*** that they (all men) are endowed by their Creator with certain inalienable rights *** (art. I, sec. 1 [declaration of rights]).

ALASKA

We, the people of Alaska, grateful to God *** establish this Constitution *** (preamble).

ARIZONA

We, the people of the State of Arizona, grateful to Almighty God for our liberties, do ordain this Constitution (preamble).

ARKANSAS

We, the people of the State of Arkansas, grateful to Almighty God (establish this Constitution) *** (preamble).

All men have a natural and indefeasible right to worship Almighty God according to the dictates of their own consciences *** (art. 2, sec. 24).

* Hearings, Prayers in Public Schools and Other Matters, Committee on the Judiciary, U. S. Senate (87th Cong., 2nd Sess.), 1962, pp. 268 et seq. See p. 55 above.

No person who denies the being of a God shall hold any office in the civil departments of this State, nor be competent to testify as a witness in any court (art. 19, sec. 1).

CALIFORNIA

We, the People of the State of California, grateful to Almighty God for our freedom, (establish this Constitution) *** (preamble).

COLORADO

We, the people of Colorado, with profound reverence for the Supreme Ruler of the Universe (establish this Constitution) *** (preamble).

CONNECTICUT

The People of Connecticut acknowledging with gratitude, the good providence of God, in having permitted them to enjoy a free government *** (establish this Constitution) (preamble).

It being the duty of all men to worship the Supreme Being, the Great Creator and Preserver of the Universe, and their right to render that worship, in the mode most consistent with the dictates of their consciences (certain rights will follow) *** (art. 7, sec. 1).

DELAWARE

Through Divine goodness, all men have by nature the rights of worshiping and serving their Creator according to the dictates of their consciences *** (preamble to constitution).

Although it is the duty of all men frequently to assemble together for the public worship of Almighty God; and piety and morality, on which the prosperity of communities depends, are hereby promoted *** (goes on to guarantee freedom of religion) (art. I, sec. 1).

FLORIDA

We, the people of the State of Florida, grateful to Almighty God for our constitutional liberty *** (establish this Constitution) (preamble).

GEORGIA

All men have the natural and inalienable right to worship God, each according to the dictates of his own conscience *** (art. 1, sec. 2-112).

*** we, the people of Georgia, relying upon the protection and guidance of Almighty God, do ordain and establish this Constitution (preamble).

HAWAII

We, the people of the State of Hawaii, grateful for Divine Guidance *** (establish this Constitution) (preamble).

IDAHO

We the people of the state of Idaho, grateful to Almighty God for our freedom (establish this Constitution) (preamble).

ILLINOIS

We, the people of the state of Illinois—grateful to Almighty God for the civil, political and religious liberty which He hath so long permitted us to enjoy, and looking to Him for a blessing upon our endeavors to secure and transmit the same unimpaired to succeeding generations *** (establish this Constitution) (preamble).

INDIANA

*** We, the People of the State of Indiana, grateful to Almighty God for the free exercise of the right to choose our form of government, do ordain this Constitution (preamble).

We declare, That all men are created equal; that they are endowed by their Creator with certain unalienable rights *** (art. 1, sec. 1).

All men shall be secured in their natural right to worship Almighty God *** (art. 1, sec. 2).

IOWA

We, the People of the State of Iowa, grateful to the Supreme Being for the blessings hitherto enjoyed, and feeling our dependence on Him for a continuation of these blessings *** (establish this Constitution) (preamble).

KANSAS

We, the people of Kansas, grateful to Almighty God for

our civil and religious privileges *** (establish this constitution) (preamble).

The right to worship God according to the dictates of conscience shall never be infringed *** (bill of rights, sec. 7.)

KENTUCKY

We, the people of the Commonwealth of Kentucky, grateful to Almighty God for the civil, political and religious liberties we enjoy *** (establish this Constitution) (preamble).

The right of worshipping Almighty God according to the dictates of their consciences (bill of rights, sec. 1).

LOUISIANA

We, the people of the State of Louisiana, grateful to Almighty God for the civil, political and religious liberties we enjoy, and desiring to secure the continuance of these blessings, do ordain and establish this Constitution (preamble).

Every person has the natural right to worship God according to the dictates of his own conscience *** (art. 1, sec 4).

MAINE

We the people of Maine *** acknowledging with grateful hearts the goodness of the Sovereign Ruler of the Universe in affording us an opportunity, so favorable to the design; and, imploring His aid and direction *** (establish this Constitution) (preamble).

All men have a natural and unalienable right to worship Almighty God according to the dictates of their own consciences *** (art. 1, sec. 3).

MARYLAND

We, the people of the State of Maryland, grateful to Almighty God for our civil and religious liberty (declare specified rights) *** (preamble to declaration of rights).

That as it is the duty of every man to worship God in such manner as he thinks most acceptable to Him, all persons are equally entitled to protection in their religious liberty *** (art. 36).

That no religious test ought ever to be required as a qualification for any office of profit or trust in this state, other than a declaration of belief in the existence of God *** (art. 37).

MASSACHUSETTS

We, therefore, the people of Massachusetts, acknowledging, with grateful hearts, the goodness of the great Legislator of the universe, in affording us, in the course of His providence, (an opportunity to form a compact); *** and devoutly imploring His direction in so interesting a design, *** (establish the Constitution) *** (preamble).

It is the right as well as the duty of all men in society, publicly, and at stated seasons to worship the Supreme Being, the great Creator and Preserver of the universe *** (declaration of rights, art. II).

As the public worship of God and instructions in piety, religion and morality, promote the happiness and prosperity of a people and the security of republican government (certain rights accrue to religious societies) *** (declaration of rights, art. III).

MICHIGAN

We, the people of the State of Michigan, grateful to Almighty God for the blessings of freedom *** (establish the Constitution) (preamble).

Every person shall be at liberty to worship God according to the dictates of his own conscience *** (art. II, sec. 3).

Religion, morality and knowledge being necessary to good government and the happiness of mankind, schools and the means of education shall forever be encouraged (art. XI, sec. 1).

MINNESOTA

We, the people of the State of Minnesota, grateful to God for our civil and religious liberty, and desiring to perpetuate its blessings *** (establish the Constitution) (preamble).

*** The right of every man to worship God according to the dictates of his own conscience shall never be infringed *** (bill of rights, art. I, sec. 16).

MISSISSIPPI

We, the people of Mississippi in convention assembled, grateful to Almighty God, and invoking his blessing on our work, do ordain and establish this constitution (preamble).

No person who denies the existence of a Supreme Being shall hold any office in this state (art. 14, sec. 265).

MISSOURI

We, the people of Missouri, with profound reverence for the Supreme Ruler of the Universe, and grateful for His goodness *** (establish this Constitution) (preamble).

That all men have a natural and indefeasible right to worship Almighty God according to the dictates of their own consciences *** (bill of rights, art. I, sec. 5).

MONTANA

We, the people of Montana, grateful to Almighty God for the blessings of liberty (establish this Constitution) *** (preamble).

NEBRASKA

We, the people, grateful to Almighty God for our freedom, *** (establish this Constitution) (preamble).

All persons have a natural and indefeasible right to worship Almighty God according to the dictates of their own consciences *** (bill of rights, art. I, sec. 4).

NEVADA

We the people of the State of Nevada grateful to Almighty God for our freedom *** (establish this Constitution) (preamble).

NEW HAMPSHIRE

Every individual has a natural and unalienable right to worship God according to the dictates of his own conscience, and reason; and no subject shall be hurt, molested, or restrained, in his person, liberty, or estate, for worshipping God in the manner and season most agreeable to the dictates of his own conscience; or for his religious profession, sentiments, or persuasions; provided he doth not disturb the public peace or disturb others in their religious worship (pt. I, art. 5).

NEW JERSEY

We, the people of the State of New Jersey, grateful to Almighty God for the civil and religious liberty which He hath so long permitted us to enjoy, and looking to Him for a blessing upon our endeavors *** (establish this Constitution) (preamble).

No person shall be deprived of the inestimable privilege of worshipping Almighty God in a manner agreeable to the dictates of his own conscience *** (art. I, sec. 3).

NEW YORK

We, the People of the State of New York, grateful to Almighty God for our Freedom, in order to secure its blessings, do establish this Constitution (preamble).

NORTH CAROLINA

We, the people of the State of North Carolina, grateful to Almighty God, the Sovereign ruler of nations, for the preservation of the American Union and the existence of our civil, political, and religious liberties, and acknowledging our dependence upon Him for the continuance of those blessings to us *** (establish this Constitution) (preamble).

That we hold it to be self-evident that all persons *** are endowed by their Creator with certain inalienable rights *** (art. 1, sec. 1).

All persons have a natural and inalienable right to worship Almighty God according to the dictates of their own consciences *** (art. 1, sec. 26).

The following classes of persons shall be disqualified for office: First, all persons who shall deny the being of Almighty God *** (art. VI, sec. 8).

NEW MEXICO

We, the people of New Mexico, grateful to Almighty God for the blessings of liberty *** (establish this Constitution) (preamble).

Every man shall be free to worship God according to the dictates of his own conscience *** (art. II, sec. 11).

NORTH DAKOTA

We, the people of North Dakota, grateful to Almighty God for the blessings of civil and religious liberty, do ordain and establish this constitution (preamble).

OHIO

We, the people of the State of Ohio, grateful to Almighty

God for our freedom *** (establish this Constitution) (preamble).

All men have a natural and indefeasible right to worship Almighty God according to dictates of their own conscience *** (bill of rights, art. I, sec. 7).

OKLAHOMA

Invoking the guidance of Almighty God, in order to secure and perpetuate the blessing of liberty (we establish this Constitution) *** (preamble).

OREGON

All men shall be secure in the Natural right, to worship Almighty God according to the dictates of their consciences (bill of rights, art. I, sec. 2).

PENNSYLVANIA

We, the people of *** Pennsylvania, grateful to Almighty God for the blessings of civil and religious liberty, and humbly invoking His guidance, do ordain and establish this Constitution (preamble).

All men have a natural and indefeasible right to worship Almighty God according to the dictates of their own consciences *** (art. I, sec. 3).

RHODE ISLAND

We, the people of the state of Rhode Island ***, grateful to Almighty God for the civil and religious liberty which He hath so long permitted us to enjoy, and looking to Him for a blessing upon our endeavors to secure and transmit the same *** (establish this Constitution) (preamble).

Whereas Almighty God hath created the mind free; and all attempts to influence it by temporal punishments or burdens, or by civil incapacitations, tend to beget habits of hypocrisy and meanness *** (art. I, sec. 3).

SOUTH CAROLINA

No person who denies the existence of a Supreme Being shall hold any office under this Constitution (art. 17, sec. 4).

We, the people of the State of South Carolina, *** grateful to God for our liberties, do ordain and establish this Constitution for the preservation and perpetuation of the same (preamble).

SOUTH DAKOTA

We, the people of South Dakota, grateful to Almighty God for our civil and religious liberties *** (establish this Constitution)(preamble).

The right to worship God according to the dictates of conscience shall never be infringed *** (art. VI, sec. 3).

TENNESSEE

That all men have a natural and indefeasible right to worship Almighty God according to the dictates of their own conscience *** (art. I, sec. 3).

No person who denies the being of God, or a future state of rewards and punishments, shall hold any office in the civil department of this State (art. IX, sec. 2).

TEXAS

Humbly invoking the blessings of Almighty God *** (we establish this Constitution) (preamble).

*** Nor shall any one be excluded from holding office on account of his religious sentiments, provided he acknowledge the existence of a Supreme Being (art. I, sec. 4).

All men have a natural and indefeasible right to worship Almighty God according to the dictates of their own consciences *** (art. I, sec. 6).

UTAH

Grateful to Almighty God for life and liberty, we *** established this Constitution (preamble).

VERMONT

That all men have a natural and unalienable right, to worship Almighty God, according to the dictates of their own consciences *** every sect or denomination of christians ought to observe the sabbath or Lord's day, and keep up some sort of religious worship, which to them shall seem most agreeable to the revealed will of God (ch. I, art. 3).

VIRGINIA

That religion or the duty which we owe to our Creator

*** can be directed only by reason and conviction, not by force or violence *** (art. I, sec. 16).

WASHINGTON

We, the people of the State of Washington, grateful to the Supreme Ruler of the Universe for our liberties, do ordain this constitution (preamble).

WEST VIRGINIA

Since through Divine Providence we enjoy the blessings of civil, political and religious liberty, we, the people of West Virginia, in and through the provisions of this Constitution, reaffirm our faith in and constant reliance upon God *** (preamble).

WISCONSIN

We, the people of Wisconsin, grateful to Almighty God for our freedom *** (establish this Constitution) (preamble).

The right of every man to worship Almighty God according to the dictates of his own conscience shall never be infringed *** (art. I, sec. 18).

WYOMING

We, the people of the State of Wyoming, grateful to God for our civil, political, and religious liberties *** (establish this constitution) (preamble).

APPENDIX C

Recognition of God in Presidential Inaugural Addresses*

GEORGE WASHINGTON, April 30, 1789

Such being the impressions under which I have, in obedience to the public summons, repaired to the present station, it would be peculiarly improper to omit in this first official act my fervent supplications to that Almighty Being who rules over the Universe, who presides in the councils of nations, and whose providential aids can supply every human defect, that His benediction may consecrate to the liberties and happiness of the people of the United States a Government instituted by themselves for these essential purposes, and may enable every instrument employed in its administration to execute with success the functions allotted to his charge. In tendering this homage to the Great Author of every public and private good, I assure myself that it expresses your sentiments not less than my own, nor those of my fellow-citizens at large less than either. No people can be bound to acknowledge and adore the Invisible Hand which conducts the affairs of men more than those of the United States.

Having thus imparted to you my sentiments as they have been awakened by the occasion which brings us together, I

* Inaugural Addresses of the Presidents of the United States (U.S. Government Printing Office, 1961). See p. 61 above.

shall take my present leave; but not without resorting once more to the benign Parent of the Human Race in humble supplication that, since He has been pleased to favor the American people with opportunities for deliberating in perfect tranquillity, and dispositions for deciding with unparalleled unanimity on a form of government for the security of their union and the advancement of their happiness, so His divine blessing may be equally conspicuous in the enlarged views, the temperate consultations, and the wise measures on which the success of this Government must depend.

GEORGE WASHINGTON, March 4, 1793

This address consisted merely of the following two paragraphs. It should be remembered that President Washington added the words "So help me, God," to the oath to which he referred.

Fellow Citizens:

I am again called upon by the voice of my country to execute the functions of its Chief Magistrate. When the occasion proper for it shall arrive, I shall endeavor to express the high sense I entertain of this distinguished honor, and of the confidence which has been reposed in me by the people of united America.

Previous to the execution of any official act of the President the Constitution requires an oath of office. This oath I am now about to take and in your presence: That if it shall be found during my administration of the Government I have in any instance violated willingly or knowingly the injunctions thereof, I may (besides incurring constitutional punishment) be subject to the upbraidings of all who are now witnesses of the present solemn ceremony.

JOHN ADAMS, March 4, 1797

. . . and, with humble reverence, I feel it to be my duty to add, if a veneration for the religion of a people who profess and call themselves Christians, and a fixed resolution to consider a decent respect for Christianity among the best recommendations for the public service, can enable me in any degree to comply with your wishes, it shall be my strenuous endeavor that this sagacious injunction of the two Houses shall not be without effect.

And may that Being who is supreme over all, the Patron of Order, the Fountain of Justice, and the Protector in all ages of the world of virtuous liberty, continue His blessing upon this nation and its Government and give it all possible success and duration consistent with the ends of His providence.

THOMAS JEFFERSON, March 4, 1801

. . . enlightened by a benign religion, professed, indeed, and practiced in various forms, yet all of them inculcating honesty, truth, temperance, gratitude, and the love of man; acknowledging and adoring an overruling Providence, which by all its dispensations proves that it delights in the happiness of man here and his greater happiness hereafter—with all these blessings, what more is necessary to make us a happy and a prosperous people?

. . . And may that Infinite Power which rules the destinies of the universe lead our councils to what is best, and give them a favorable issue for your peace and prosperity.

THOMAS JEFFERSON, March 4, 1805

. . . I shall need, too, the favor of that Being in whose hands we are, who led our fathers, as Israel of old, from their native land and planted them in a country flowing with all the necessaries and comforts of life; who has covered our infancy with His providence and our riper years with His wisdom and power, and to whose goodness I ask you to join in supplications with me that He will so enlighten the minds of your servants, guide their councils, and prosper their measures that whatsoever they do shall result in your good, and shall secure to you the peace, friendship, and approbation of all nations.

JAMES MADISON, March 4, 1809

But the source to which I look for the aids which alone can supply my deficiencies is in the well-tried intelligence and virtue of my fellow-citizens, and in the counsels of those representing them in the other departments associated in the care of the national interests. In these my confidence will under every difficulty be best placed, next to that which we have all been encouraged to feel in the guardianship and guidance of that Almighty Being whose power regulates the destiny of nations, whose blessings have been so conspicuously dispensed to this rising Republic, and to whom we are bound to address our devout gratitude for the past, as well as our fervent supplications and best hopes for the future.

JAMES MADISON, March 4, 1813

. . . The impressions on me are strengthened by such an evidence that my faithful endeavors to discharge my arduous duties have been favorably estimated, and by a consideration of the momentous period at which the trust has been renewed. From the weight and magnitude now belonging to it I should be compelled to shrink if I had less reliance on the support of an enlightened and generous people, and felt less deeply a conviction that the war with a powerful nation, which forms so prominent a feature in our situation, is stamped with that justice which invites the smiles of Heaven on the means of conducting it to a successful termination.

JAMES MONROE, March 4, 1817

. . . Relying on the aid to be derived from the other departments of the Government, I enter on the trust to which I have been called by the suffrages of my fellow-citizens with my fervent prayers to the Almighty that He will be graciously pleased to continue to us that protection which He has already so conspicuously displayed in our favor.

JAMES MONROE, March 5, 1821

. . . In surmounting, in favor of my humble pretensions, the difficulties which so often produce division in like occurrences, it is obvious that other powerful causes, indicating the great strength and stability of our Union, have essentially contributed to draw you together. That these powerful causes exist, and that they are permanent, is my fixed opinion; that they may produce a like accord in all questions touching, however remotely, the liberty, prosperity, and happiness of our country will always be the object of my most fervent prayers to the Supreme Author of All Good.

... With full confidence in the continuance of that candor and generous indulgence from my fellow-citizens at large which I have heretofore experienced, and with a firm reliance on the protection of Almighty God, I shall forthwith commence the duties of the high trust to which you have called me.

JOHN QUINCY ADAMS, March 4, 1825

In compliance with an usage coeval with the existence of our Federal Constitution, and sanctioned by the example of my predecessors in the career upon which I am about to enter, I appear, my fellow citizens, in your presence and in that of Heaven to bind myself by the solemnities of religious obligation to the faithful performance of the duties alloted to me in the station to which I have been called.

... and knowing that "except the Lord keep the city the watchman waketh but in vain," with fervent supplications for His favor, to His overruling providence I commit with humble but fearless confidence my own fate and the future destinies of my country.

ANDREW JACKSON, March 4, 1829

... And a firm reliance on the goodness of that Power whose providence mercifully protected our national infancy, and has since upheld our liberties in various vicissitudes, encourages me to offer up my ardent supplications that He will continue to make our beloved country the object of His divine care and gracious benediction.

ANDREW JACKSON, March 4, 1833

Finally, it is my most fervent prayer to that Almighty Being, before whom I now stand, and who has kept us in His hands from the infancy of our Republic to the present day, that He will so overrule all my intentions and actions and inspire the hearts of my fellow-citizens that we may be preserved from dangers of all kinds and continue forever a united and happy people.

MARTIN VAN BUREN, March 4, 1837

So sensibly, fellow-citizens, do these circumstances press themselves upon me that I should not dare to enter upon my path of duty did I not . . . above all . . . permit myself humbly to hope for the sustaining support of an ever-watchful and beneficial Providence.

. . . Beyond that I only look to the gracious protection of the Divine Being whose strengthening support I humbly solicit, and whom I fervently pray to look down upon us all. May it be among the dispensations of His providence to bless our beloved country with honors and with length of days. May her ways be ways of pleasantness and all her paths be peace!

WILLIAM HENRY HARRISON, March 4, 1841

. . . We admit of no government by divine right, believing that so far as power is concerned the Beneficent Creator has made no distinction amongst men; that all are upon an equality, and that the only legitimate right to govern is an express grant of power from the governed.

I deem the present occasion sufficiently important and solemn to justify me in expressing to my fellow-citizens a profound reverence for the Christian religion and a thorough conviction that sound morals, religious liberty, and a just sense of religious responsibility are essentially connected with all true and lasting happiness; and to that good Being who has blessed us by the gifts of civil and religious freedom, who watched over and prospered the labors of our fathers and has hitherto preserved to us institutions far exceeding in excellence those of any other people, let us unite in fervently commending every interest of our beloved country in all future time.

JAMES K. POLK, March 4, 1845

In assuming responsibilities so vast I fervently invoke the aid of that Almighty Ruler of the Universe in whose hands are the destinies of nations and of men to guard this Heaven-favored land against the mischiefs which without His guidance might arise from an unwise public policy. With a firm reliance upon the wisdom of Omnipotence to sustain and direct me in the path of duty which I am appointed to pursue, I stand in the presence of this assembled multitude of my countrymen to take upon myself the solemn obligation "to the best of my ability to preserve, protect, and defend the Constitution of the United States."

Confidently relying upon the aid and assistance of the coordinate departments of the Government in conducting our public affairs, I enter upon the discharge of the high duties which have been assigned me by the people, again humbly supplicating that Divine Being who has watched over and protected our beloved country from its infancy to the present hour to continue His gracious benedictions upon us, that we may continue to be a prosperous and happy people.

ZACHARY TAYLOR, March 5, 1849

In conclusion I congratulate you, my fellow-citizens, upon the high state of prosperity to which the goodness of Divine Providence has conducted our common country. Let us invoke a continuance of the same protecting care which has led us from small beginnings to the eminence we this day occupy, and let us seek to deserve that continuance by prudence and moderation in our councils, by well-directed attempts to assuage the bitterness which too often marks unavoidable differences of opinion, by the promulgation and practice of just and liberal principles, and by an enlarged patriotism, which shall acknowledge no limits but those of our own widespread Republic.

FRANKLIN PIERCE, March 4, 1853

. . . The energy with which that great conflict was opened and, under the guidance of a manifest and beneficent Providence the uncomplaining endurance with which it was prosecuted to its consummation were only surpassed by the wisdom and patriotic spirit of concession which characterized all the counsels of the early fathers.

. . . It is with me an earnest and vital belief that as the Union has been the source, under Providence, of our prosperity to this time, so it is the surest pledge of a continuance of the blessings we have enjoyed, and which we are sacredly bound to transmit undiminished to our children.

. . . It must be felt that there is no national security but in the nation's humble, acknowledged dependence upon God and His overruling providence.

. . . Standing, as I do, almost within view of the green slopes of Monticello, and, as it were, within reach of the tomb of Washington, with all the cherished memories of the past gathering around me like so many eloquent voices of exhortation from heaven, I can express no better hope for my country than that the kind Providence which smiled upon our fathers may enable their children to preserve the blessings they have inherited.

JAMES BUCHANAN, March 4, 1857

. . . Convinced that I owe my election to the inherent love for the Constitution and the Union which still animates the hearts of the American people, let me earnestly ask their powerful support in sustaining all just measures calculated to perpetuate these, the richest political blessings which Heaven has ever bestowed upon any nation.

I shall now proceed to take the oath prescribed by the Constitution, whilst humbly invoking the blessing of Divine Providence on this great people.

ABRAHAM LINCOLN, March 4, 1861

. . . Intelligence, patriotism, Christianity, and a firm reliance on Him who has never yet forsaken this favored land are still competent to adjust in the best way all our present difficulty.

. . . *You* have no oath registered in heaven to destroy the Government, while *I* shall have the most solemn one to "preserve, protect, and defend it."

ABRAHAM LINCOLN, March 4, 1865

Neither party expected for the war the magnitude or the duration which it has already attained. . . . Both read the same Bible and pray to the same God, and each invokes His aid against the other. It may seem strange that any men should dare to ask a just God's assistance in wringing their bread from the sweat of other men's faces, but let us judge not, that we be not judged. The prayers of both could not be answered. That of neither has been answered fully. The Almighty has His own purposes. "Woe unto the world because of offenses; for it must needs be that offenses come, but woe to that man by whom the offense cometh." If we shall suppose that American slavery is one of those offenses which, in the providence of God, must needs come, but which, having continued through His appointed time, He now wills to remove, and that He gives to both North and South this terrible war as the woe due to those by whom the offense came, shall we discern therein any departure from those divine attributes which the believers in a living God always ascribe to Him? Fondly do we hope, fervently do we pray, that this mighty scourge of war may speedily pass away. Yet, if God wills that it continue until all the wealth piled by the bondsman's two hundred and fifty years of unrequited toil shall be sunk, and until every drop of blood drawn with the lash shall be paid by another drawn with the sword, as was said three thousand years ago, so still it must be said "the judgments of the Lord are true and righteous altogether."

With malice toward none, with charity for all, with firmness in the right as God gives us to see the right, let us strive on to finish the work we are in, to bind up the nation's wounds, to care for him who shall have borne the battle and for his widow and his orphan, to do all which may achieve and cherish a just and lasting peace among ourselves and with all nations.

ULYSSES S. GRANT, March 4, 1869

In conclusion I ask patient forbearance one toward another throughout the land, and a determined effort on the part of every citizen to do his share toward cementing a happy union; and I ask the prayers of the nation to Almighty God in behalf of this consummation.

ULYSSES S. GRANT, March 4, 1873

Under Providence I have been called a second time to act as Executive over this great nation.

. . . Rather do I believe that our Great Maker is preparing the world, in His own good time, to become one nation, speaking one language, and when armies and navies will be no longer required.

RUTHERFORD B. HAYES, March 5, 1877

Looking for the guidance of that Divine Hand by which the destinies of nations and individuals are shaped, I call upon you, Senators, Representatives, judges, fellow-citizens, here and everywhere, to unite with me in an earnest effort to secure to our country the blessings, not only of material prosperity, but of justice, peace and union—a union depending not upon the constraint of force, but upon the loving devotion of a free people; "and that all things may be so ordered and settled upon the best and surest foundations that peace and happiness, truth and justice, religion and piety, may be established among us for all generations."

JAMES A. GARFIELD, March 4, 1881

. . . Let our people find a new meaning in the divine oracle which declares that "a little child shall lead them," for our own little children will soon control the destinies of the Republic.

My countrymen, we do not now differ in our judgment concerning the controversies of past generations, and fifty years hence our children will not be divided in their opinions concerning our controversies. They will surely bless their fathers and their fathers' God that the Union was preserved, that slavery was overthrown, and that both races were made equal before the law.

I shall greatly rely upon the wisdom and patriotism of Congress and of those who may share with me the responsibilities and duties of administration, and, above all, upon our efforts to promote the welfare of this great people and their Government I reverently invoke the support and blessings of Almighty God.

GROVER CLEVELAND, March 4, 1885

. . . And let us not trust to human effort alone, but humbly acknowledging the power and goodness of Almighty God, who presides over the destiny of nations, and who has at all times been revealed in our country's history, let us invoke His aid and His blessing upon our labors.

BENJAMIN HARRISON, March 4, 1889

. . . Entering thus solemnly into convenant with each other, we may reverently invoke and confidently expect the favor and help of Almighty God—that He will give to me wisdom, strength, and fidelity, and to our people a spirit of fraternity and a love of righteousness and peace.

. . . God has placed upon our head a diadem and has laid at our feet power and wealth beyond definition or calculation. But we must not forget that we take these gifts upon the condition that justice and mercy shall hold the reins of power and that the upward avenues of hope shall be free to all the people.

GROVER CLEVELAND, March 4, 1893

. . . Deeply moved by the expression of confidence and personal attachment which has called me to this service, I am sure my gratitude can make no better return than the pledge I now give before God and these witnesses of unreserved and complete devotion to the interests and welfare of those who have honored me.

It can not be doubted that our stupendous achievements as a people and our country's robust strength have given rise to heedlessness of those laws governing our national health which we can no more evade than human life can escape the laws of God and nature.

Above all, I know there is a Supreme Being who rules the affairs of men and whose goodness and mercy have always followed the American people, and I know He will not turn from us now if we humbly and reverently seek His powerful aid.

WILLIAM MCKINLEY, March 4, 1897

In obedience to the will of the people, and in their presence, by the authority vested in me by this oath, I assume the arduous and responsible duties of President of the United

States, relying upon the support of my countrymen and invoking the guidance of Almighty God. Our faith teaches that there is no safer reliance than upon the God of our fathers, who has so singularly favored the American people in every national trial, and who will not forsake us so long as we obey His commandments and walk humbly in His footsteps.

. . . Illiteracy must be banished from the land if we shall attain that high destiny as the foremost of the enlightened nations of the world which, under Providence, we ought to achieve.

. . . This is the obligation I have reverently taken before the Lord Most High. To keep it will be my single purpose, my constant prayer; and I shall confidently rely upon the forbearance and assistance of all the people in the discharge of my solemn responsibilities.

WILLIAM MCKINLEY, March 4, 1901

Intrusted by the people for a second time with the office of President, I enter upon its administration appreciating the great responsibilities which attach to this renewed honor and commission, promising unreserved devotion on my part to their faithful discharge and reverently invoking for my guidance the direction and favor of Almighty God.

. . . As heretofore, so hereafter will the nation demonstrate its fitness to administer any new estate which events devolve upon it, and in the fear of God will "take occasion by the hand and make the bounds of freedom wider yet."

THEODORE ROOSEVELT, March 4, 1905

My fellow citizens, no people on earth have more cause to be thankful than ours, and this is said reverently, in no spirit of boastfulness in our own strength, but with gratitude to the Giver of Good who has blessed us with the conditions which have enabled us to achieve so large a measure of well-being and of happiness.

WILLIAM H. TAFT, March 4, 1909

Having thus reviewed the questions likely to recur during my administration, and having expressed in a summary way the position which I expect to take in recommendations to Congress and in my conduct as an Executive, I invoke the considerate sympathy and support of my fellow-citizens and the aid of the Almighty God in the discharge of my responsible duties.

WOODROW WILSON, March 4, 1913

. . . The feelings with which we face this new age of right and opportunity sweep across our heartstrings like some air out of God's own presence, where justice and mercy are reconciled and the judge and the brother are one.

. . . I summon all honest men, all patriotic, all forward-looking men, to my side. God helping me, I will not fail them, if they will but counsel and sustain me!

WOODROW WILSON, March 5, 1917

. . . We are being forged into a new unity amidst the fires that now blaze throughout the world. In their ardent heat we shall, in God's Providence, let us hope, be purged of faction and division, purified of the errant humors of party and of private interest, and shall stand forth in the days to come with a new dignity of national pride and spirit.

. . . I pray God I may be given the wisdom and the prudence to do my duty in the true spirit of this great people.

WARREN G. HARDING, March 4, 1921

Standing in this presence, mindful of the solemnity of this occasion, feeling emotions which no one may know until he senses the great weight of responsibility for himself, I must utter my belief in the divine inspiration of the founding fathers. Surely there must have been God's intent in the making of this new-world Republic.

One cannot stand in this presence and be unmindful of the tremendous responsibility. The world upheaval has added heavily to our tasks. But with the realization comes the surge of high resolve, and there is reassurance in belief in the God-given destiny of our Republic. If I felt that there is to be sole responsibility in the Executive for the America of tomorrow I should shrink from the burden. But here are a hundred millions, with common concern and shared responsibility, answerable to God and country. The Republic summons them to their duty, and I invite co-operation.

I accept my part with single-mindedness of purpose and humility of spirit, and implore the favor and guidance of God in His Heaven. With these I am unafraid, and confidently face the future.

I have taken the solemn oath of office on that passage of Holy Writ wherein it is asked: "What doth the Lord require of thee but to do justly and to love mercy, and to walk humbly with thy God?" This I plight to God and country.

CALVIN COOLIDGE, March 4, 1925

. . . Peace will come when there is realization that only under a reign of law, based on righteousness and supported by the religious conviction of the brotherhood of man, can there by any hope of a complete and satisfying life. Parchment will fail, the sword will fail, it is only the spiritual nature of man that can be triumphant.

. . . All owners of property are charged with a service. These rights and duties have been revealed, through the conscience of society, to have a divine sanction.

. . . America seeks no earthly empire built on blood and force. No ambition, no temptation, lures her to thought of foreign dominions. The legions which she sends forth are armed, not with the sword, but with the cross. The higher state to which she seeks the allegiance of all mankind is not of human, but of divine origin. She cherishes no purpose save to merit the favor of Almighty God.

HERBERT HOOVER, March 4, 1929

This occasion is not alone the administration of the most sacred oath which can be assumed by an American citizen. It is a dedication and consecration under God to the highest office in service of our people. I assume this trust in the humility of knowledge that only through the guidance of Almighty Providence can I hope to discharge its ever increasing burdens.

. . . I ask the help of Almighty God in this service to my country to which you have called me.

FRANKLIN D. ROOSEVELT, March 4, 1933

In such a spirit on my part and on yours we face our common difficulties. They concern, thank God, only material things.

In this dedication of a Nation we humbly ask the blessing of God. May He protect each and every one of us. May he guide me in the days to come.

FRANKLIN D. ROOSEVELT, January 20, 1937

While this duty rests upon me I shall do my utmost to speak their purpose and to do their will, seeking Divine guidance to help us each and every one to give light to them that sit in darkness and to guide our feet into the way of peace.

FRANKLIN D. ROOSEVELT, January 20, 1941

We do not retreat. We are not content to stand still. As Americans, we go forward, in the service of our country, by the will of God.

FRANKLIN D. ROOSEVELT, January 20, 1945

The Almighty God has blessed our land in many ways. He has given our people stout hearts and strong arms with which to strike mighty blows for freedom and truth. He has given to our country a faith which has become the hope of all peoples in an anguished world.

So we pray to Him now for the vision to see our way clearly—to see the way that leads to a better life for ourselves and for all our fellow men—to the achievement of His will, to peace on earth.

HARRY S. TRUMAN, January 20, 1949

. . . We believe that all men are created equal because they are created in the image of God.

From this faith we will not be moved.

These differences between communism and democracy do

not concern the United States alone. People everywhere are coming to realize that what is involved is material well-being, human dignity, and the right to believe in and worship God.

Steadfast in our faith in the Almighty, we will advance toward a world where man's freedom is secure.

To that end we will devote our strength, our resources, and our firmness of resolve. With God's help, the future of mankind will be assured in a world of justice, harmony and peace.

DWIGHT D. EISENHOWER, January 20, 1953

My friends, before I begin the expression of those thoughts that I deem appropriate to this moment, would you permit me the privilege of uttering a little private prayer of my own. And I ask that you bow your heads.

Almighty God, as we stand here at this moment my future associates in the executive branch of government join me in beseeching that Thou will make full and complete our dedication to the service of the people in this throng, and their fellow citizens everywhere.

Give us, we pray, the power to discern clearly right from wrong, and allow all our words and actions to be governed thereby, and by the laws of this land. Especially we pray that our concern shall be for all the people regardless of station, race and calling.

May cooperation be permitted and be the mutual aim of those who, under the concepts of our Constitution, hold to differing political faiths; so that all may work for the good of our beloved country and Thy glory. Amen.

In the swift rush of great events, we find ourselves groping to know the full sense and meaning of these times in which we live. In our quest of understanding, we beseech God's guidance.

This faith defines our full view of life. It establishes, beyond debate, those gifts of the Creator that are man's inalienable rights, and that make all men equal in His sight.

It is because we, all of us, hold to these principles that the political changes accomplished this day do not imply turbulence, upheaval or disorder. Rather this change expresses a purpose of strengthening our dedication and devotion to the precepts of our founding documents, a conscious renewal of faith in our country, and in the watchfulness of a Divine Providence.

This is the hope that beckons us onward in this century of trial. This is the work that awaits us all, to be done with bravery, with charity, and with prayer to Almighty God.

DWIGHT D. EISENHOWER, January 21, 1957

Before all else, we seek, upon our common labor as a nation, the blessings of Almighty God. And the hopes in our hearts fashion the deepest prayers of our whole people.

And so the prayer of our people carries far beyond our own frontiers, to the wide world of our duty and our destiny.

JOHN F. KENNEDY, January 20, 1961

. . . For I have sworn before you and Almighty God the same solemn oath our forebears prescribed nearly a century and three quarters ago.

. . . And yet the same revolutionary beliefs for which our forebears fought are still at issue around the globe—the belief that the rights of man come not from the generosity of the state but from the hand of God.

. . . With a good conscience our only sure reward, with history the final judge of our deeds, let us go forth to lead the land we love, asking His blessing and His help, but knowing that here on earth God's work must truly be our own.

President Abraham Lincoln's Proclamation of a Day of National Humiliation, Fasting and Prayer, April 30, 1863*

Whereas the Senate of the United States, devoutly recognizing the supreme authority and just government of Almighty God in all the affairs of men and of nations, has by a resolution requested the President to designate and set apart a day for national prayer and humiliation:

And whereas it is the duty of nations as well as of men to own their dependence upon the overruling power of God; to confess their sins and transgressions in humble sorrow, yet with assured hope that genuine repentance will lead to mercy and pardon; and to recognize the sublime truth, announced in the Holy Scriptures and proven by all history, that those nations only are blessed whose God is the Lord:

And, insomuch as we know that by His divine law nations, like individuals, are subjected to punishments and chastisements in this world, may we not justly fear that the awful calamity of civil war which now desolates the land may be but a punishment inflicted upon us for our presumptuous sins, to the needful end of our national reformation as a whole people? We have been the recipients of the choicest bounties of Heaven. We have been preserved, these many

* Complete Works of Lincoln (Nicolay and Hay, eds.) (1905), VIII, 235. See p. 113 above.

years, in peace and prosperity. We have grown in numbers, wealth and power as no other nation has ever grown. But we have forgotten God. We have forgotten the gracious hand which preserved us in peace, and multiplied and enriched and strengthened us, and we have vainly imagined, in the deceitfulness of our hearts, that all these blessings were produced by some superior wisdom and virtue of our own. Intoxicated with unbroken success, we have become too self-sufficient to feel the necessity of redeeming and preserving grace, too proud to pray to the God that made us:

It behooves us, then, to humble ourselves before the offended Power, to confess our national sins, and to pray for clemency and forgiveness:

Now, therefore, in compliance with the request, and fully concurring in the views, of the Senate, I do by this my proclamation designate and set apart Thursday the 30th day of April, 1863, as a day of national humiliation, fasting, and prayer. And I do hereby request all the people to abstain on that day from their ordinary secular pursuits, and to unite at their several places of public worship and their respective homes in keeping the day holy to the Lord, and devoted to the humble discharge of the religious duties proper to that solemn occasion. All this being done in sincerity and truth, let us then rest humbly in the hope authorized by the divine teachings, that the united cry of the nation will be heard on high, and answered with blessings no less than the pardon of our national sins, and the restoration of our now divided and suffering country to its former happy condition of unity and peace.

In witness whereof, I have hereunto set my hand and caused the seal of the United States to be affixed.

Done at the City of Washington, this thirtieth day of March, in the year of Our Lord one thousand eight hundred and sixty-three, and of the Independence of the United States the eighty-seventh.

ABRAHAM LINCOLN

Index

INDEX

INDEX